BOSTON in the GOLDEN AGE of SPIRITUALISM

SÉANCES, MEDIUMS & IMMORTALITY

DEE MORRIS

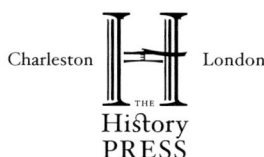

Charleston · London

The History Press

Published by The History Press
Charleston, SC 29403
www.historypress.net

Copyright © 2014 by Dee Morris
All rights reserved

Front cover: "Mrs. Conant (1862–1875)." Albumen silver print of a photograph by William H. Mumler. *Courtesy of the J. Paul Getty Museum, Los Angeles.*
Back cover: *Courtesy of the Library of Congress.*

First published 2014

Manufactured in the United States

ISBN 978.1.62619.587.5

Library of Congress CIP data applied for.

Notice: The information in this book is true and complete to the best of our knowledge. It is offered without guarantee on the part of the author or The History Press. The author and The History Press disclaim all liability in connection with the use of this book.

All rights reserved. No part of this book may be reproduced or transmitted in any form whatsoever without prior written permission from the publisher except in the case of brief quotations embodied in critical articles and reviews.

CONTENTS

Acknowledgements	5
Introduction	7
1. The Coming of the Light	11
2. A Definition of Purpose	36
3. The Rejection of Boundaries	58
4. A Tale of Two Towns	71
5. The Truth Behind the Illusion	92
Epilogue	119
Bibliography	121
Index	125
About the Author	127

ACKNOWLEDGEMENTS

Many thanks are due to Ryan Hayward, who examined images, offered insights into Boston history, took beautiful photographs and offered his computer skills. Thanks go out to Dora St. Martin, director of the Malden Public Library, for sharing her wealth of knowledge about spiritualism and her technical expertise. Members of the Greater Boston Spiritualist Church provided context in which to place the movement. Reverend Mary DiGiovanni was especially helpful in explaining the role and importance of mediums. Joan Quigley and other community activists offered perceptive insights into their local history. Gillian Lang from Historic Boston tracked down an image, while Karen Shafts at the Boston Public Library went the extra mile. Ellen Knight at the Winchester Archives and Sara Lundberg at the Arlington Historical Society combed through their collections. Finally, Tabitha Dulla at The History Press has been a very patient and knowledgeable guide through this process.

Spiritualist newspapers and materials can be difficult to locate. The International Association for the Preservation of Spiritualist and Occult Periodicals (http://www.iapsop.com) is a nonprofit organization that maintains a rich archive of these publications. Having the *Banner of Light* constantly available, minus the usual dimness of microfilm, was not only crucial but also created the impression that I was reading the news as it happened.

INTRODUCTION

During the last half of the nineteenth century, a new revelation opened up the minds and hearts of a diverse group of Americans. Spiritualism, the belief in the soul's immortality and the reality of communicating with the departed, conquered the fear of death. Men and women were encouraged to investigate the manifestations of spirits. They participated in séances or meetings in which a medium conveyed messages to them from the beyond. There was no hierarchy to obey, no orthodoxy to follow and no hell to dread. Spiritualism also pushed aside the anxiety of floundering about in a hostile universe. Spirits were always on hand to offer guidance; nevertheless, believers had to exercise discernment and common sense when dealing with these immortals.

The movement began in the village of Hydesville, New York, situated in the western part of the state. In March 1848, two young girls, Katie and Margaret Fox, insisted that the frequent noises emanating from the walls of their bedroom were being made by a spirit. These knockings, also called rappings, were said to be the work of a traveling peddler who had been murdered in the house one year before. They responded with their own raps and gradually developed a system of communication. Other spirits joined in the daily "conversations." The younger girls convinced their much-older sister, Leah, of the truth of their experiences. Word spread into the community, creating such interest that the sisters demonstrated the phenomenon before a paying audience. More events followed, which launched not only their own careers but also a national craze.

Introduction

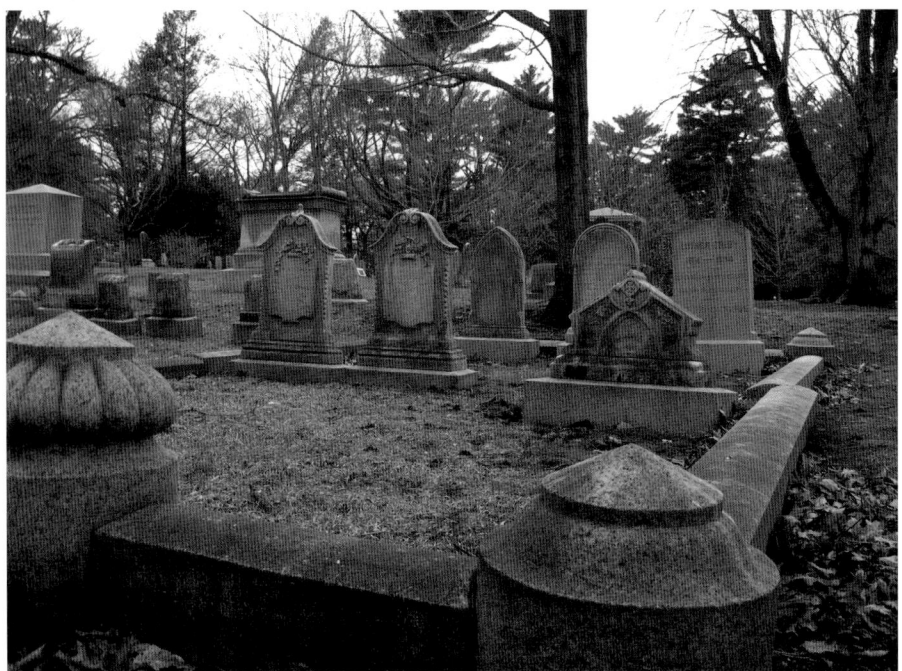

Fanny Conant and her friends enjoy eternal rest in the same lot at Forest Hills Cemetery. *Ryan Hayward.*

In 1850, Boston embraced spiritualism with enthusiasm. Although New York City was very active in this movement, the first spiritualist newspaper was published in Boston. Within a few years, numerous clairvoyants were engaged in healing the sick, testing the presence of spirits and relaying messages. The *Banner of Light*, emerging in the 1850s, was the preeminent and longest-running spiritualist weekly journal in the country. When the city was physically enlarged by filling in the surrounding tidal flats, spiritualists fanned out to the newly built neighborhoods. The magnificent First Spiritual Temple established an iconic presence in the Back Bay. Many believers commuting back and forth to work from their homes in the suburbs attended lectures and séances in the city. Spiritualism was an intrinsic part of the Boston fabric.

I first became aware of Victorian spiritualists when planning a walking tour at Forest Hills Cemetery in Jamaica Plain. This famous garden cemetery just south of Boston was consecrated in 1848, the same year as the Hydesville rappings took place. Stopping on Honeysuckle Path, I noticed a theme. Several monuments were carved with a variation of one phrase: "passed on," "passed to the higher life" or "passed away." A bit of research indicated that this motto was a favorite saying in the spiritualist community. Who were these people?

Fanny Conant's lot represents the mother lode of Boston spiritualism. Mrs. Conant, two editors of the *Banner of Light*, her clairvoyant brother and her Native American protégé are buried here. The nearby stones belong to spiritualist friends and neighbors. These believers belonged to a vibrant group that dealt with the question of immortality every day of their lives. Most of their histories have been forgotten, fading away along with the lettering on their marble memorials.

These interesting people deserve to be viewed within the context of their world. The *Banner* provided such a lens because it chronicled not only the séances and events but also the personalities of the mediums and participants. International doings and news from across the country were included, but the prime spotlight remained on Boston and surrounding towns. During the fifty-plus years that spiritualism was such a force locally, it attracted a wide following, including some performers who were frauds. The following vignettes and stories illustrate the diverse spectrum of believers, authentic professionals and unrepentant pretenders who were active during this era.

Chapter 1
THE COMING OF THE LIGHT

In the 1850s, local spiritualists were in the process of defining their beliefs. People were discovering spirit communication while still dealing with organized religion. It was the decade to look within, to discard what was no longer important and to embrace a new view of life.

THE BLAZING COMET: LaRoy Sunderland (1804–1885)

Boston was home to one of the most mercurial personalities ever to embrace spiritualism. LaRoy Sunderland, a brilliant but restless soul, had the habit of waxing and waning in his support for causes ranging from traditional religion to abolition. In 1850, he published the *Spiritual Philosopher*, a newspaper that he proclaimed was the first spiritualist journal on earth. His married daughter, Mrs. Margaretta S. Cooper, had the distinction of becoming Boston's first public medium.

LaRoy's craving to be noticed began while he was still a boy in Rhode Island. His teenage enthusiasm for religion inspired him to become an itinerant Methodist preacher in the 1820s. During his first sermon preached in Massachusetts, some members of the congregation were so profoundly moved by his voice that a few fell prostrate on the floor. Others beat their chests in sorrow, while a number ecstatically clapped their hands.

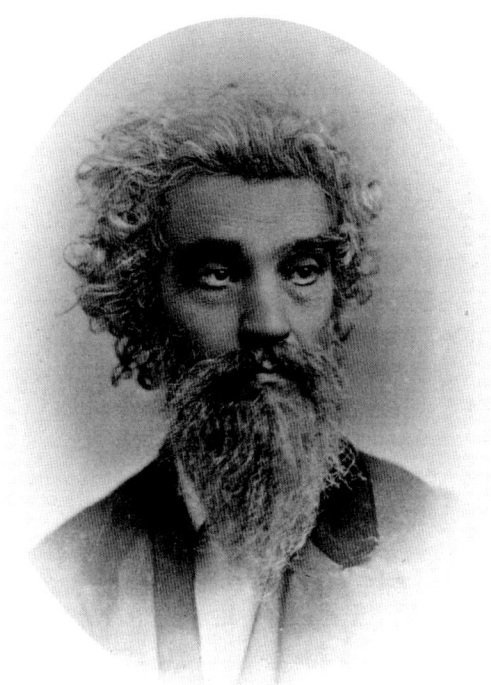

LaRoy Sunderland, an intense perfectionist, communicated with the spirits of his sons. *Massachusetts Historical Society.*

The reverend wondered if these Pentecostal displays were signs of God's approval. It soon occurred to him that he possessed an extraordinary talent. Sunderland would later describe this ability as the power of "Fascination," which caused a subject to lose self-control upon being mesmerized. In his early days, he successfully experimented with hypnosis.

The young clergyman plunged into family life. In December 1828, while working in Malden, just north of Boston, he married the talented Mehitable Ewins (1807–1901), who was drawn to his intensity. Margaretta, their first daughter, arrived in 1829. In a few years, after recuperating from severely straining his vocal chords in the 1830s, Sunderland moved his growing family to New York, where he spent a decade wrangling with the Methodist Episcopal Church over its proslavery stance. When he was defrocked over the issue, he immediately became mired in a personal crisis of faith. The former minister felt vindicated when he published his view that orthodox religion was riddled with hypocrisy.

In 1844, the self-designated "Dr." Sunderland was lecturing in Lynn on his latest interest, which he dubbed Pathetism, a "science" closely related to mesmerism. Assuming the role of a healer, Sunderland promised that he could cure ailments without inflicting pain in the process. Liberal papers, such as Boston's *Chronotype*, reported that in one public session, the amateur physician had successfully dissolved a cancerous tumor. By the end of the decade, he had delivered sixty-two lectures in the Masonic Temple on Tremont Street, plus written a manual. Sunderland was primed for his grand immersion into spiritualism.

Two years after the Fox sisters unveiled their experiments in spirit rappings in 1848, Bostonians were talking about the new phenomenon. The Sunderland family was by then living in a twenty-room home located in Charlestown, a city independent from Boston. LaRoy, embarking on his own experiments, was confident that he was communicating with his deceased young sons. With great satisfaction, he stated, "We have had some peculiar manifestations from the spirits of our children during the night, which have brought us to consciousness from sound sleep." He was gratified to learn from one of his spirit boys that they were still continuing to grow into manhood.

Ghostly knocks began to reverberate off the sides of rooms, the back of his desk and from the top of the china cupboard. As the spirit presences infiltrated the dining room, it became evident that other members of the family were endowed with clairvoyant abilities. Margaretta, now a married woman, and her younger sister, Sarah, could answer spirits' questions, access music coming from unattended guitars and cause heavy furniture to relocate. Sunderland was aware that, up to this time, other documented cases of spirit contact took place only after people had contacted the Fox sisters to act as intermediaries with the invisible world.

Sunderland incorporated his experiences into his professional life. Spiritualism and hands-on healing were the two avenues he used to cure the afflicted. He put together an office on Boston's Court Street near the water. Here, his clients, aware of his spirit connections, made appointments to find relief from imperfect sight, St. Vitus Dance, deafness and palpitations of the heart. He sold his own publications, plus those of his good friend Andrew Jackson Davis, a pioneer in the movement. Mehitable, his wife, built a reputation by using the restorative powers of magnetism, a popular belief that powerful, sometimes curative, electrical currents flowed between people. She also supplied her female clientele with the approved versions of shoulder braces and abdominal supporters.

Sunderland wanted a bigger audience. He rented a nearby hall where he delivered lectures about the Hydesville knockings and hosted free "Conversations on Spiritual Subjects." Then he directed his energies toward producing the *Spiritual Philosopher*, which he printed at his office and charged two

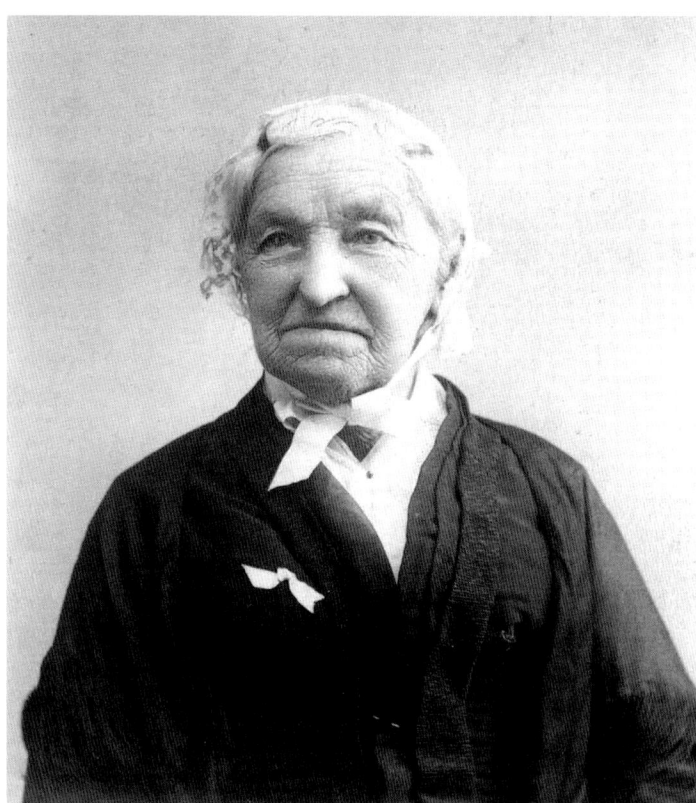

Mehitable Sunderland was an extraordinary healer interested in magnetic currents. *Hyde Park Historical Society.*

dollars per year for a subscription, paid in advance. He flooded the pages with vignettes about his own work and experiences. Completely convinced that he had been given the key to unlocking the door to happiness, Sunderland boasted about his excursions into the heavenly realm in addition to congratulating himself on the exquisiteness of his publication. In August 1850, he wrote, "It is our design, and we think we have the means at command, for making the *Spiritual Philosopher* so <u>attractive</u>, that a very large number will read it; and once read, we hope it may be the means of <u>good</u> to the souls and bodies of men."

In later years, Emma Hardinge, an astute chronicler of early spiritualism, suggested that Sunderland "was transported beyond the plane of calm and rational observation." His dedication to "truth and good" was amply tinged with self-absorption. Yet he was proud to be the father of a woman with a direct line to the beyond.

Even before she turned twenty, Margaretta S. Cooper (1829–1898) was a seasoned veteran of the Boston lecture scene. She was a skilled musician and singer who warmed up the audience before her father performed. Her friends and subsequent clients described her as being very ladylike, well dressed and having long dark brown curls. When she married John D. Cooper Jr., a young man working in the hotel trade, in 1849, they boarded in her parents' home. Her father must have seen some promise in his son-in-law because he described Cooper as a skillful practitioner of the art of Pathetism. These heightened words probably meant that John was only an assistant. The Coopers' one daughter, Ada, was born in 1850, about the time that John faded away from the family history.

While still living in Charlestown, Mrs. Cooper's psychic abilities expanded. She loved to sit by the fireplace, rocking to sleep her two-month-old daughter while raps emanated from within the cradle. The baby's bed would often be moved several inches, seemingly transported by unseen hands. Margaretta, on occasion, would be entranced and write down messages but could not remember what had been communicated when she awoke. She held séances for friends and a few paying clients. Although she was self-effacing, her one extravagance was her love of colorful jewelry. Some attendees wondered if she purchased her trinkets with the money they paid her.

As her customer base increased, so did the number of spirits that visited the sessions. In October 1850, her father wrote an editorial in which he boasted that there were upward of three hundred invisible beings present per séance. Margaretta was so popular, he declared, that everyone in the neighborhood had come repeatedly to witness the wonderful communications taking place on Salem Street.

By the turn of the New Year in 1851, the family relocated to a larger home and office on Boston's Eliot Street, where Margaretta received the public every day except Sunday. Her séances, now more sophisticated, attracted notables such as antislavery champions William Lloyd Garrison and Wendell Phillips. William C. Nell, an author and Garrison's African American colleague, found her sincere as well as insightful.

Keeping her long-range plan in mind, she started to schedule sessions for private groups in their respective homes. The most unusual evening took place at the residence of clients related to Dr. George Parkman, who was murdered in 1849. This wealthy physician had been cut down—literally—by another Harvard faculty member, John Webster. Given the fact that the victim was an upper-class merchant, the sordid event, which led to the trial and execution of Webster, dominated polite conversation for months. The doctor's surviving relatives were not only interested in contacting their departed kinsman but also wanted to reach out to deceased European friends. They wrote all their questions in French, a language unfamiliar to Margaretta. She later stated that some friendly bilingual spirits inspired her to deliver responses in a Parisian dialect. This intervention by the immortals boosted her self-confidence.

While Mrs. Cooper prospered, her father fell victim to a hoax in 1851. The trap was set by a columnist from the *New York Express* who sent LaRoy a gut-wrenching counterfeit letter from an imaginary Phebe Newell, whose fictitious friend, Mary Ellen Perkins, had taken her own life out of despair. "Mrs. Newell" enclosed one dollar in order to receive a prompt response from Sunderland about Mary Ellen's status in the spirit world. Had she been saved? In good faith, LaRoy wrote back that the spirit of Mary was standing by his side and was sending affectionate greetings to her elderly friend. Her eternal happiness had been guaranteed. The subterfuge, complete with a reprint of the letters, was gleefully broadcast in several Boston and regional newspapers. Sunderland was convinced that some vicious spirits had masterminded the event. Despite having received warnings from Margaretta that not every communication could be taken on face value, Sunderland insisted that, because he was acting in good faith, the spirits should protect him from anything deceptive. He began the descent into his usual self-righteous indignation.

Believers in the local community distanced themselves. Disillusioned, Sunderland poured out his views in *A Book of Human Nature* (1853), which ended with a bitter denunciation of his latest interest. He bullied local mediums, such as Mrs. Hayden, whom he accused of being a "damned spirit." Spiritualists, he decided, were either cheats or out to ruin him. The movement had to be repudiated because it was not perfect.

When his newspaper failed, his volatile personality created turmoil within the home. By the end of the decade, the Sunderland marriage had been terminally fractured. Mehitable filed for divorce in 1859 on the grounds that her husband neglected to provide financial support for her well-being. He said that she refused to live with him. After she settled in Hyde Park, Boston's most southern suburb, the former Mrs. Sunderland gained respect as a healer and midwife, eventually becoming the first physician in town. LaRoy concentrated on his medical practice in his constant search for perfection.

Margaretta gained traction as the public began to see her as a professional who was free from the influence of her troubled father. Much more confident now, she refused to take responsibility for the truthfulness of any spirit contacted during a session. She believed that hostile audiences attracted undeveloped or angry beings from the beyond, while sincere seekers of truth drew in helpful invisibles. A positive environment was the key to a fruitful meeting. These two basic concepts served her well and also built a foundation for the many mediums who would soon engage in the business. Her success stimulated the community to research spiritualism informally.

As spirit circles in private homes became more frequent, mediums proliferated. Mrs. Helen Leeds from Carver Street rented rooms to other spiritualists, such as George Redman. He enjoyed the informal social reunions held every month in her front parlor. Miss Burbank and Mrs. Langford shared their insights when they co-hosted gatherings combined with light refreshments. Spiritualism was gaining attention and even notoriety, depending on the personality of the clairvoyant. Another arena being impacted was the stronghold of orthodox religion.

THE COUPLE WITH A CONSCIENCE: ALONZO E. (1821–1889) AND SARAH JANE NEWTON (1820–1893)

The Newtons were exemplary members of the Edwards Congregational Church—until they were forbidden to pursue the most soul-satisfying experience of their lives. Communicating with departed spirits was condemned as one of the devil's most insidious snares. In 1853, Alonzo and Sarah Jane challenged the authority of this Bible-centered assembly by writing a public explanation of their reasons to support the "wonderful works of God" that were being revealed everyday through spiritualism. Their enlightenment came at a cost but transformed them into explorers on the brink of eternity.

Affectionately known as Lonnie, Newton embodied the American ideal of a self-made man who overcomes obstacles. His difficult birth in Marlborough, New Hampshire, in 1821 branded him as the most fragile of eight children. A strong will enabled him to persevere through years of poverty, which were intensified by his father's early demise. After joining his widowed mother and sisters in Lowell, a booming textile center on the Merrimack River, he worked in the mills until his health was compromised. Then his older sister's death forced him to be the sole breadwinner for the family. Newton vowed that his life was going to amount to more than coping with one calamity after another.

By 1844, Newton was editing Boston's *Temperance Standard*, a reform journal, and was happily engaged to Sarah Jane Emery, a young Bostonian who became his devoted soul mate. Over five years later, the couple joined the Edwards Church, which performed outreach among the downtrodden of the neighborhood outlined by Lowell and Causeway Streets. Alonzo was grateful to be making a decent living as a proofreader at *Snow's Pathfinder Railway Guide*. Sarah Jane loved caring for their three children in a modest home on Beacon Hill's West Cedar Street. Life was pleasantly unexciting—until Alonzo encountered spiritualism.

A colleague at the *Pathfinder* in early 1852 could not stop raving about a séance that he had attended at Hayward Place. Newton finally accepted the invitation to experience the raps for himself but privately thought that he would find only trickery. The evening at Mrs. M.B. Hayden's home attracted a crowd of believers and skeptics who strained to hear the faint smattering of knocks. Newton and his disappointed companion arranged for a private session, which reverberated with a cascade of loud noises, thus suggesting the presence of several beings. At another séance several days later, Alonzo received detailed messages supposedly being transmitted by his long-dead father. Newton still had doubts, although he was impressed. He needed to talk this over with his wife.

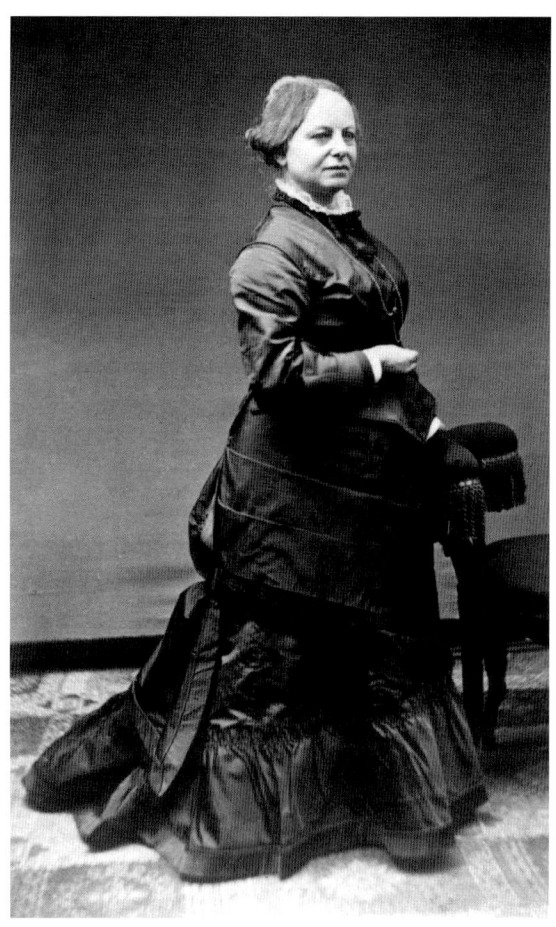

Sarah Jane Newton welcomed friendly spirits into her home, where they helped care for the children. *Arlington Historical Society.*

If nothing else than to put to rest Lonnie's questions, Sarah Jane volunteered to sit in on a circle directed by Mrs. Hayden. The results were spectacular. Bursts of enthusiastic raps enveloped the table and ricocheted off the walls. The medium could not keep up with the many communications flowing from all the departed relatives vying to be heard. Most startling was the final announcement. A light-drenched immortal predicted that Mrs. Newton would become a clairvoyant possessing extraordinary abilities.

One Sunday, Reverend Pond of the Edwards Church preached an unusual sermon based on the "Ministry of Angels." He suggested that after death, Christians were permitted to become the guardians of loved ones still on earth. Coincidentally, Sarah Jane was aware of the ghostly forms of departed church members standing in the sanctuary. She greeted a luminous being, apparently the pastor's deceased mother, who came over to encourage her to act on the minister's words. Once back in the tranquility of their house, the Newtons pondered the similarities between the homily and the central belief of spiritualism. They decided to use their residence as a testing ground. Sarah Jane opened her mind to the invisible visitors that she intuited were waiting in the background. She prayed that she was not doing something that would harm her family.

Whether in the kitchen, dining room or bedroom, Mrs. Newton perceived hundreds of beings surrounded by light. Their voices were audible to her ears alone, much to the wonderment of her husband. These friends from the beyond taught her how to prepare nutritious meals for the children and to implement suggestions concerning their health, such as allowing fresh air into the bedrooms. Nothing was extreme or fantastic. Spirits even watched over the little ones during the dark hours of the night. After many sessions, the Newtons were left with a final piece of wisdom: the universe followed the eternal law of progression, meaning that the human spirit was immortal and deserved nurturing equal to the care lavished on body and mind. All these revelations were delivered by the "angels" that were really departed men and women enjoying a higher level of awareness.

Such joyful experiences had to be shared. During a private interview with their minister, the couple disclosed everything but were cautioned by him not to broadcast the story. But they did, and there were veiled threats of repercussions. The Newtons took action by writing their position paper, *The "Ministry of Angels" Realized*. Hundreds of pamphlets were printed. Each member of the congregation received a copy, although some refused to read it. On the other hand, the couple had numerous friends who wanted to comprehend this formal rejection of orthodoxy. After being criticized by the church elders, the Newtons answered with a request for a formal dismissal. That was not forthcoming, but the council did charge that the troublemakers were guilty of insubordination and denial of doctrine. Excommunication was imminent. In a cheeky response, Alonzo and Sarah Jane reminded the church that dismissal was unnecessary because they had already left. Within weeks, the Edwards community voted to disband due to insolvency.

Mrs. Newton proceeded to learn everything that she could from her invisible teachers. Even during the turmoil with the church, she was already regaling Alonzo with the marvels happening at their own fireside. His colleagues at the Devonshire Street publishing house were captivated by the stories of her mediumistic abilities, and soon everyone was spreading the word. John T. Trowbridge, a frequent contributor to the *Carpet Bag* magazine located on an upper floor, asked to interview Sarah Jane because he was curious about spiritualism.

His first impression was that this petite housewife possessed an extremely empathetic personality. She seemed almost childlike, which, he admitted, was an interesting change from the more polished style of the local spirit-rapping mediums. When the two first sat together, he watched her close her eyes, draw her breath in sharply and pass into a half-waking state, although she never fully lost consciousness. She mentioned that his father's spirit was present, but that tidbit was not pursued. Trowbridge planned more visits, based on his instinct as a writer that he was watching an average woman evolve into a clairvoyant.

Trowbridge had the satisfaction of observing Sarah Jane hone her psychometric skills, which involved reading the characters of complete strangers by placing a lock of their hair or a personal item between the palms of her hands. He tested her by enclosing mementos from three different associates in separate envelopes. Holding the papers, Mrs. Newton described each person accurately and then became influenced by her spirit friends who added more information. Trowbridge came to understand that she experienced visions that were inspired by immortals and not fabricated by her own imagination.

By 1854, Alonzo wanted to offer the community a forum in which spiritualism could be discussed and evaluated rationally. In his view, evidence of communicating with spirits was on the rise, as more men and women were drawn to explore these developments for themselves. Newton envisioned editing a newspaper that, free from specific dogmas, could chart the evolution of the new philosophy. Sarah Jane urged him to approach their friend Allen Putnam, a minister-turned-spiritualist, for the funds necessary to float the enterprise. By March 1855, her husband had rented office space on Franklin Street in the heart of town and was devoting all his energies to publishing the *New England Spiritualist*. His financial backers assured the public that Alonzo

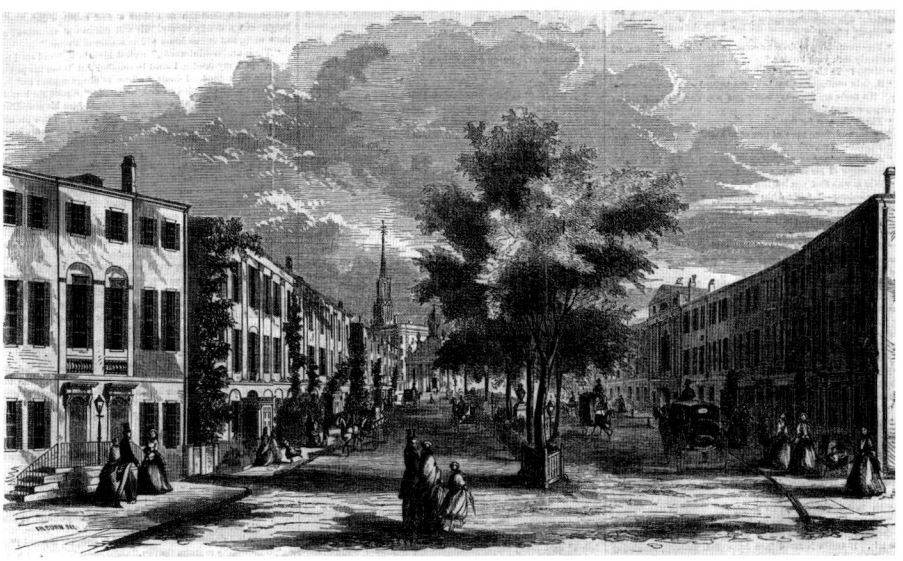

Franklin Street in the 1850s supported a mix of progressive businesses. *Author's collection.*

would "admit nothing into his columns that [would] be offensive to good taste, sound morals, or pure religion." The resulting weekly was professionally tolerant toward all shades of opinion. Bela Marsh, a spiritualist friend and preeminent publisher of progressive periodicals, moved in downstairs. The block became known as a mecca for independent thought.

Across the Atlantic, Charles Dickens expected to detest Alonzo's newspaper before he even leafed through one issue. His first brush with spiritualism had occurred in 1852, when Maria Hayden, the medium who had converted the Newtons, had dazzled London with her séances. Despite being ridiculed by the press, she made a great impact on the fashionable middle class. Dickens was particularly annoyed that she charged a fee for her services. Still fuming three years later, he chose to spew his vitriol on her fellow Bostonian. His scathing review was written for *Household Words,* a weekly magazine that combined fiction with essays about any topic that caught Dickens's fancy or annoyed him. He dismissed Yankees, in general, as "having the eyes of a mole and the swallow of a hippopotamus." Newton, in his august opinion, was not only myopic and gullible but also an uneducated rustic who was easily duped by any self-styled healer or mystic looking to make some money.

Unperturbed, Alonzo was buoyed up by his wife during her frequent stops on Franklin Street to proofread the copy. He closely followed her progress as a channel for the spirits, frequently writing about her as "Mrs. N." His favorite vignette occurred one Saturday in 1856 when Sarah Jane whispered that two immortals were approaching, their arms twined around a third wearing an old-fashioned mob cap. That being stepped forward to convey words of affection and sympathy meant to reassure both of them that they were being protected. With tears streaming down her face, Sarah Jane recounted the experience to her husband since he was not able to participate in her visions. The next week, Alonzo showed her a picture of Elizabeth Fry, a deceased English reformer who had been devoted to serving destitute children and prisoners. Receiving confirmation that this was indeed the apparition from the earlier night, Newton joyfully acknowledged that Sarah Jane never failed to provide the most tangible proof of spirit existence.

She was the spiritual center that anchored him even after he had to surrender his beloved paper in 1858 due to health issues and a downwardly spiraling economy. He worked with S.B. Brittan on the *Spiritual Age*, a New York publication, but lack of revenue forced him to leave the helm of a business that had been his passion.

The family then moved across the Charles River to enjoy country living in Cambridgeport followed by an extended stay in Somerville, where they could breathe in the fresh air of Prospect Hill. John Trowbridge, the writer, joined their family circle in the small house on Munroe Street, where he soon fell in love with and married Cornelia, the Newtons' beautiful daughter. By the end of the decade, Newton was invited to be a guest columnist for the next paper to emerge, the vibrant *Banner of Light*. Alonzo's voice was too important to be silenced. Boston spiritualism could never repay the Newtons for their groundbreaking treatise about the value of spirit revelation. As the *Banner* would comment decades later, "*The 'Ministry of Angels' Realized* became one of the standard works of the new movement."

Getting the Word Out: The *Banner of Light* (1857–1907)

The *Banner of Light* was the longest-running spiritualist newspaper of the nineteenth century. It was a rallying point for the Boston community, New England and every supporter scattered throughout the States. At times viewed as too tolerant, maybe even naïve, there was no other paper that represented the breadth of American spiritualism so completely. It was a

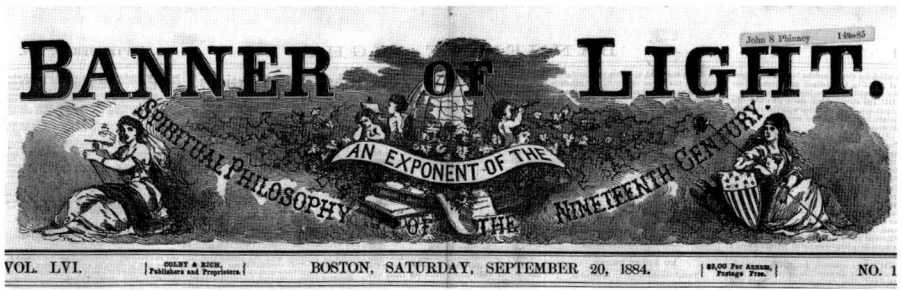

This iconic news sheet informed and encouraged Boston spiritualists for over fifty years. *Author's collection.*

point of pride that the pages presented some of the most controversial topics found in a changing society. In April 1857, the paper stated, "While carefully refraining from identifying ourselves with the different 'isms' of the day, we prefer rather to roll onward with the car of Progress than to be crushed under its wheels, and therefore, esteem it a duty we owe to ourselves and our readers to investigate calmly and candidly any new Truth or theory." The weekly sheet boasted from its first issue that it would present a buffet of "Romance Literature and General Intelligence." Featuring melodramatic fiction, often about perils encountered in a treacherous world, it set out to charm rather than to confront. Tucked into the third paragraph of the first editorial was its unique mission statement: "We shall pursue an even, straightforward course," respecting the phenomenon of spiritualism.

Three mortals were inspired by a band of dedicated spirits to make the *Banner* a tangible reality. Luther Colby, the principal editor, and William Berry, a young entrepreneur, were the driving forces. Fanny Conant, a spectacular public medium, contributed her psychic insights and abilities.

The Experienced Veteran: Luther Colby (1814–1894)

Before the *Banner* was even a faint concept, Luther Colby had spent the majority of his life fascinated with the power of the printed word. His first assignment as a printer's apprentice in Exeter, New Hampshire, involved preparing an edition of the Bible. He loved the appearance of the book but had no interest in the contents, which he considered to be stifling. Coming to

Boston in 1836, Luther secured a job at the *Boston Post,* a leading daily paper, where he excelled at every position from compositor to editor. He thought of retiring after twenty years but had no strategy in place for the future. In November 1855, he casually attended a séance at Mrs. Stearns's home on Cambridge Street. When he received an unexpected message that a new career would be opening up, he knew that he had just turned the page to the most fulfilling chapter of his life.

THE ENERGETIC BUSINESSMAN: WILLIAM BERRY (1825–1862)

In the 1850s, William Berry arrived in Boston with the objective of making a good living as a printer. Quick witted and sometimes rash, he did not have the temperament to wait for the world to come to him. William was soon employed downtown, where he met Luther Colby. In the evenings, he left the city to relax in the working-class neighborhood of North Cambridge next to the Alewife River. Berry, a young widower, soon married Jane N. Ross, whose brother was a professional medium. After witnessing a couple of séances, William became a firm believer who zealously probed every aspect of spiritualism. Every Wednesday, he invited twenty people to his house, where his brother-in-law would contact the spirits of their departed friends. The arrangement was perfect—until James announced his departure for Cuba in 1855. Berry started searching for a trustworthy medium to fill the void.

THE PSYCHIC CENTER: FANNY CONANT (1831–1875)

In the fall of 1851, Mrs. Frances Conant and her husband, John, were newlyweds renting rooms in Boston's North End, where she hoped to become a successful dressmaker. Always delicate, Fanny soon fell into a decline that threatened to be terminal. John panicked enough to procure a morphine-based prescription from an alcoholic physician. When administered, the concoction plunged his wife into a deep stupor for several days. It seemed almost miraculous when she suddenly regained consciousness, her body shaking from a series of involuntary shocks similar to excessive charges from an electric battery. Other near-death experiences convinced Fanny to seek a cure apart from traditional medicine. She consulted Anna Richardson, a fifteen-year-old spiritualist, who encouraged her to open up her mind to Dr. John Dix Fisher, a departed physician. To Fanny's amazement, he predicted her return to health, as well as her new role as a gifted medium. He offered to guide her future efforts, which, he promised, would help thousands of people. She trusted him because he knew her secret. As a sickly child, she had conversed with "angels." Within months, Mrs. Conant and her husband were living on Hanover Street, where her séances, under the guidance of Dr. Fisher, were gaining recognition.

The Trio Comes Together

Luther Colby introduced Mrs. Conant to William Berry, who had made it known that he was in the market for a new medium to conduct séances in his home. She had limited success at her first session in North Cambridge. Her spirit guide, Dr. Fisher, was unable to recommend any medication that would cure a sick young girl. Berry, nevertheless, had the wisdom to understand that this new clairvoyant was extraordinary.

In the winter of 1855, Fanny accepted William's offer to become a medium-in-residence. Luther Colby's visits increased as he was drawn to the séances and William's hospitality. One Wednesday evening, Dr. Fisher's spirit announced that an important collaboration was on the horizon. The *Banner of Light*, given this title by a group of dedicated immortals, was going to debut as the most significant newspaper to come out of Boston. Colby and Berry were to be partners and managers, while Fanny would provide the psychic center. The long-awaited connection with the spirit world had been made. Colby was fond of saying that, at this moment, a new *Banner* of truth was "unfurled."

A Dynamic Way to Communicate with the Beyond: The Public Circles

By the fall of 1857, Fanny's séances had taken on a different appearance. She was officially a member of the staff, presiding over public sessions in which a diverse array of spirits connected with an equally eclectic audience.

William Berry offered to make transcriptions when it became evident that some of the spirit visitors were not known to anyone attending the séances. These narratives were printed "as is" every week, which meant, for example, that the bad grammar, slang and individual bias expressed by the immortals was retained. At one meeting, the spirit of Mary Ann Gleason, once from Hillsborough, New Hampshire, spoke about "angels meeting me at my coming." But spirit William Wheeler, in earthly life a common drunkard, started his monologue with "Hi, yah! This is a whole team and a couple of donkeys thrown in! I'd like to know how I come here!"

The Message Department soon became the most popular section of the paper, eliciting glowing reviews from the many readers who were pleased to be able to verify the names and stories of the departed. Some secular newspapers criticized Mrs. Conant for creating an obscene "spirit telegraph" that mimicked the one in the temporal world. The *Boston Courier* printed many letters from Professor Felton of Harvard, who characterized Mrs. Conant as an ignorant woman uttering wild statements. Fanny knew that she would have to overcome every low attempt to undermine her efforts.

After three years, Colby and Berry were confident that they had been able to keep the *Banner* from foundering on the "shoals of Fanaticism." In fact, Luther stated, "We have labored under many difficulties, most of which have ceased to annoy us."

Harvard and the Investigators

Local spiritualism had its share of powerful detractors. Most vocal were the conservative ministers and editors who took every opportunity to rail against this upstart philosophy. Harvard College then joined the fray when the "evil" of spiritualism was detected on the Cambridge campus. A divinity school student was the culprit.

The Scholarly Maverick: Frederick L.H. Willis (1830–1914)

April 1857 proved to be a terrible month for Frederick L.H. Willis, who was in the process of completing his initial ministerial studies. His scholastic career disintegrated before his eyes when he was unceremoniously "suspended"—actually expelled. His crime was practicing deception while holding a séance. Faculty members thought the charge of fraud would be more damning than reprimanding him for engaging in an unapproved activity.

Three years earlier, Willis had barely heard of spiritualism. Along with his professors, he dismissed it as a theatrical delusion fit only for the uneducated. Willis had a more pressing issue to resolve. He had been ordered by physicians to take a sea voyage in order to regain his shattered health. Once on the ocean, however, he feared that he was prone to hallucinations. Rappings echoed throughout his stateroom each time he reminisced about two acquaintances who had recently died. The quest for wellness became an endurance test.

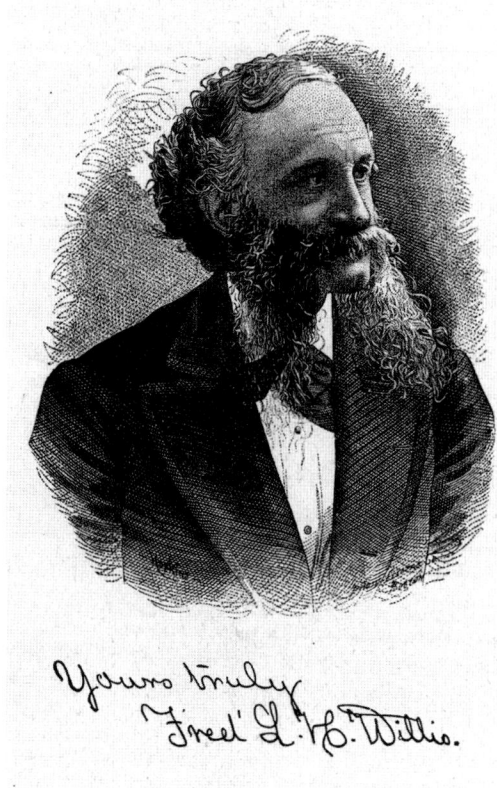

Harvard could not come to terms with having a medium on campus. Fred Willis was expelled, causing much discomfort in Cambridge. *Boston Public Library.*

When he returned to Boston, he talked with practicing spiritualists and discovered that he might be a medium. He was interested in trying out his nascent powers, which led to applying his own efforts to contact spirit friends. As his skills increased and his confidence grew, he held circles in Cambridge, Boston, Salem and other locales. The tipping of tables, rappings and other assorted signs of spirit activity occurred with such frequency that they became topics of interest, especially given his reputation as a Harvard intellectual. He was able to access the spirits of Byron, Shelley and poets from antiquity. In his presence, camellias, roses and ferns suddenly appeared out of thin air. It was wonderfully exciting. The Harvard faculty heard rumors that these sessions were taking place in private homes, but the institution did not act because Willis maintained his high grades.

The ordeal began when a relative of Professor Henry Eustis asked Willis to invite the teacher to a few séances in an effort to soften the man's negative viewpoint. At this time, Willis was testing the potential spirit use of musical instruments. He also had the habit of crossing one leg over the other, leaving his left foot to dangle. In one meeting, with Eustis present, two drumsticks were tapping out an intricate interpretation of the rhythm of "Hail Columbia" on a mid-sized drum. Suddenly, the teacher reached his hands under the table, grabbed the student's foot and announced that Willis was guilty of producing the syncopated beat.

Despite protestations of his innocence, Willis went back to Cambridge sick in heart and body. The professor wasted no time in publicly denouncing him and bringing him up on charges before the faculty and president. Within days, Willis was informed that he was no longer welcome at the divinity school. Because the sensational situation unfolded at Harvard, it was deemed newsworthy. Conservative papers defended the expulsion, while a few dailies took the college to task. The *Banner* praised Willis as a God-fearing scholar who had been vilified for his beliefs. Willis benefited from the notoriety because he had become a "martyr" to the cause of spiritualism.

The Boston Investigating Committee: The Hunger to Debunk

Just weeks after the Willis debacle, Dr. Henry Gardner, a respected spiritualist organizer, was thrown into the thick of a contest with Harvard College. The formal contest was set for June 25–27 and was initiated by the editor of the *Boston Courier*, who used his antipathy toward spiritualism to boost the paper's circulation. He threw out a challenge to anyone who could produce verifiable spiritualist phenomena under predetermined conditions. The prize was $500, to be awarded for authentic manifestations that included table-tipping and rappings. Dr. Gardner felt obliged to accept, pledging that he would recruit some reputable mediums to hold séances in the presence of men approved by the *Courier*. The "disinterested" parties chosen by the paper included Professors Peirce, Agassiz and Horsford, plus Dr. B.A. Gould, a

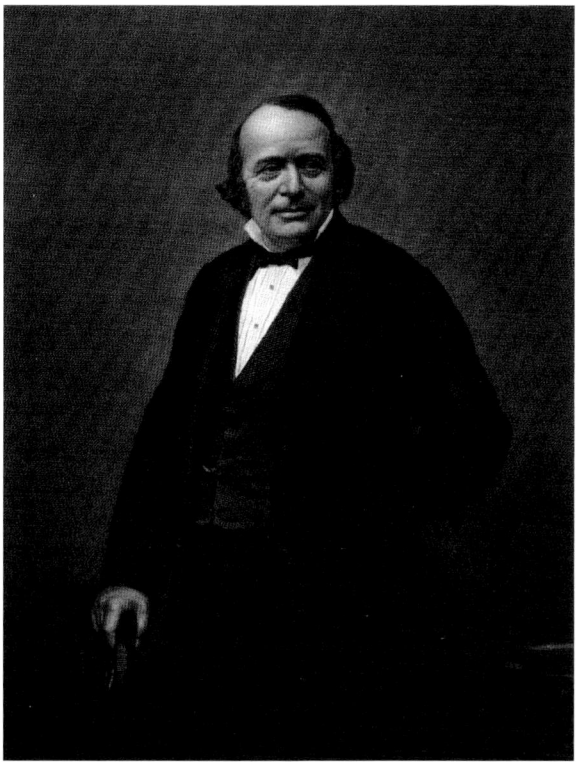

Professor Agassiz from Harvard tested the abilities of several mediums to make a valid spirit connection. *Author's collection.*

Cambridge scientist. Gardner enlisted his own spectators: Alvin Adams, a spiritualist businessman; Reverend Allen Putnam, a Harvard graduate; and Major Raines from New York. He also invited a reporter from the *Boston Traveler* and Dr. Luther Bell, former superintendent of the McLean Lunatic Asylum, as more neutral observers. The tests encompassed a marathon of three days.

Gardner made it quite clear that the money did not entice him. If the spiritualists were to prevail, he asked that the *Courier* pick up the costs and the rental of chambers at the Albion building on Tremont Street. Two of his celebrity psychics were Mrs. Brown, formerly Leah Fox, and her sister, Katherine, whose travel expenses had to be covered. His local choices were Mrs. Kendrick; J.V. Mansfield, who was making a name for himself by answering sealed letters; and George Redman, a young medium of twenty-two. The Davenport brothers were also summoned. They specialized in producing manifestations after being tied with ropes and shut inside a freestanding cabinet. That duo was controversial.

The Albion's apartment number twelve was approved. In the center of the room, a raised wooden platform held a pine table and chairs. The setting guaranteed that vibrations caused by any rap would carry well. Dr. Bell, Mr. Adams, the Fox sisters and Major Raines formed a circle. Everyone else sat on single seats and sofas. All was still. Finally, taps of varied intensity were heard. Mrs. Brown exclaimed that she felt a soft touch on her neck, perhaps from a spirit hand. The women were asked to stand on stools and then to mount chairs. Raps continued no matter where the mediums placed themselves. Professor Peirce posed questions that the spirits did not like because he received inconclusive taps for answers. Dr. Agassiz was requested to take a seat in the circle but angrily refused, much to the annoyance of Dr. Gardner, who would later observe that the air of hostility emanating from the Harvard scientist must have intimidated the immortals. The invisibles fell silent for the remainder of the afternoon. Rather surprisingly, Leah Fox Brown was more sympathetic toward Agassiz. She knew that since the professor was preconditioned to being mesmerized, his perambulations around the room were his attempt to keep free of outside influences. The opening event was disappointing to the spiritualists and somewhat gratifying to the challengers.

The next session was worse. Professor Agassiz hovered near Mr. Redman, the young medium who was trying to channel the departed. Suddenly, the pine table lurched forward violently as Redman announced that the spirits were pleading for cooperation. Then silence descended as the temperature in the room increased because the windows were sealed. When Alvin Adams persuaded Redman to adjourn to a more ventilated chamber, they experienced a torrent of rappings. During their absence, the test room remained unnaturally quiet. After several hours, the mediums unanimously declined to continue in such a negative environment. The Fox sisters departed the next morning after deciding that they had endured enough unpleasantness. Mr. Mansfield became the focus of Professor Horsford's attention. Known for his ability to "read" the contents of sealed letters, he failed to connect with the beyond or to understand the sealed texts. To this point, the spiritualists had made a very poor showing.

During the final evening session, the Davenport brothers' manifestations were tested. The professors, after binding the young men with ropes, placed the boys in a large, freestanding cabinet containing rough benches and an array of musical instruments. According to the mediums' affidavits, spirit musicians were to play tunes while the Davenports remained trussed up. They would then be released from their bondage by the same invisibles. Dr. Peirce insisted on sitting behind the subjects and holding a banjo. The door was bolted shut, and the lights were extinguished. Silence prevailed as everyone held their breaths, and the boys remained tied. Nothing happened. No music was heard.

The *Courier* editor dismissed the meetings as silly, tedious and morally dishonest. An official statement from the professors warned the community "against this contaminating influence [of spiritualism] which surely tends

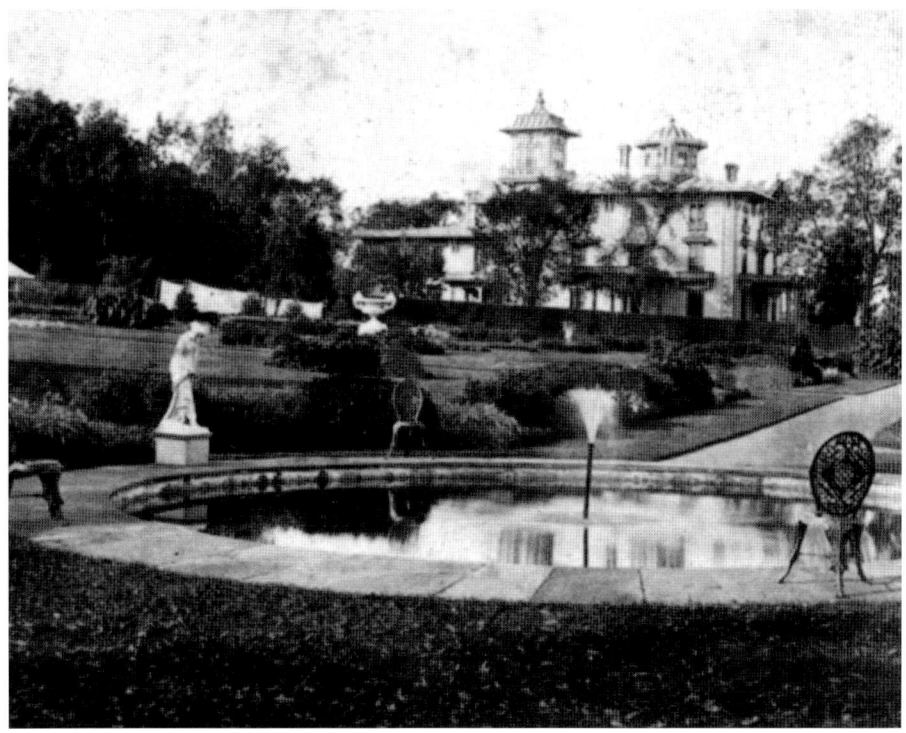

Alvin Adams, owner of the Adams Express company, was a wealthy spiritualist who eventually owned a magnificent estate in Watertown. *Author's collection.*

to lesson the truth of men and the purity of women." Mr. Redman, on the spiritualist side, reminded the public that communicating with the beyond was impossible in such a confusing and antagonistic environment. Dr. Gardner privately absorbed the expenses and got back to organizing lectures.

The Firebrand Who Believed: John Pierpont (1785–1866)

Spiritualism was the culmination of Reverend John Pierpont's search for truth. His wholehearted interest in spirit communication during the 1850s seemed odd for a man grounded in the here and now. Known for years as a provocateur dedicated to social reform, he had published antislavery poems in defense of universal freedom and lobbied for the fair treatment of

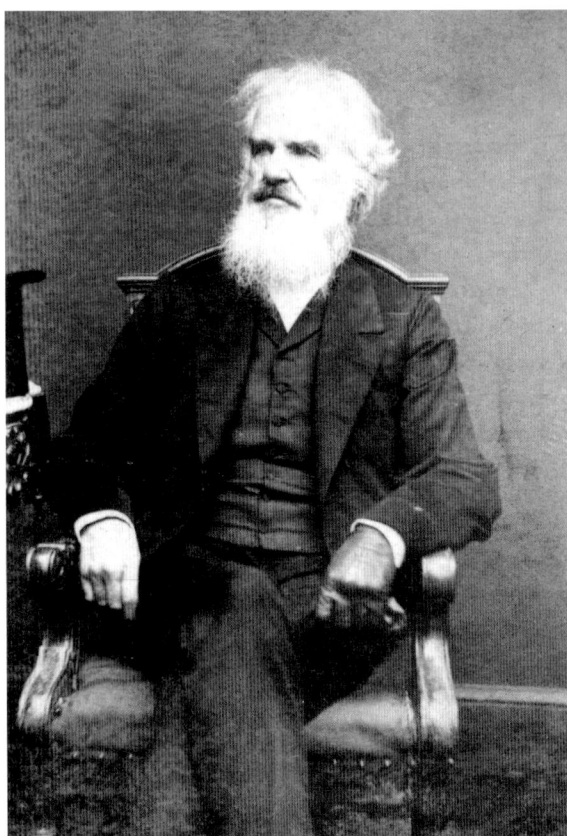

John Pierpont, grandfather of J.P. Morgan, wrote letters to his mentor, the spirit of William Ellery Channing. *Author's collection.*

debtors. More moderate colleagues had accused him of being an extremist when he crusaded for temperance. Over six feet tall and ramrod straight, Pierpont followed his heart wherever it led.

His own life had been an uneven patchwork of choices. After graduating from Yale College in 1804, John worked as a private tutor in the South, where he saw the brutality of slavery firsthand. He married Mary Sheldon Lord, his fourth cousin, in 1810 and was admitted to the Massachusetts State Bar. His faltering law practice pushed him into a retail venture, which then failed due to a downturn in the economy. Upon completing Harvard Divinity School, he accepted a position at Boston's elite Hollis Street Church in 1819. His community activism rankled many in the conservative congregation, finally causing a terminal rift that ended his twenty-plus years of service. Mary had, all the while, devoted herself to raising their six children. By 1845, Pierpont was delivering intense homilies in Troy, New York, while he studied mesmerism. He believed a skilled practitioner could use this God-given tool to relieve the sufferings of the afflicted. When he was well into his sixties, John was invited to minister to a Massachusetts community located on the banks of the Mystic River. Mary, burdened with long-term health issues, looked forward to living in the bucolic town slightly north of Boston.

The Pierponts built their spacious house in the tree-filled neighborhood of West Medford. Although they were congratulating themselves on being semi-retired, they should have remembered that one of their children often had "issues." In 1850, their second son arrived with his wife, Millicent, and their two children in tow. He was on a mission. James, a young man with big dreams, set off alone to work as a photographer in California during the gold rush. His parents opened their hearts and home to Millicent, an infant and a very active toddler. The next year, a freak tornado roared through this section of Mystic Street, demolishing a portion of the Pierponts' roof in its fury. No one was injured, but John suspected that this was a sign of future upheavals.

James lost his business in a San Francisco fire, forcing him to return filled with discontent. Millie then endured a difficult pregnancy only to have the baby succumb to complications in 1855. Her husband left Medford permanently to join his brother in Savannah, where he continued his new career as a composer. "Jingle Bells" remains his legacy. Talented yet unreliable, he was absent when his mother died, and his wife passed away a few months later in 1856.

Trying to cope with his own grief, the elder Pierpont was determined to ease the sense of loss that threatened to overwhelm his granddaughter and, to a much lesser degree, her younger brother. He reached into his past to refresh his knowledge of hypnotism. Most likely, he selected his library as the proper location for the treatment of the highly responsive Mary Augusta. After she closed her eyes to concentrate on his words, John held his hands above her so that their magnetic warmth could flow over her body. She entered a calm trance-like state during which she was able to carry on pleasant conversations without any trace of fear. The therapy succeeded due to her trust in him and her openness to hypnotic suggestion.

Pierpont was unexpectedly introduced to spirit messages through Mary Augusta's enhanced sensitivity. It had been evident for several weeks that she was using her own will power to become entranced. This self-induced condition caused her voice to deepen into the tones of a mature adult. She began to expound on theological questions that were far beyond the understanding of a ten-year-old. John found himself discussing the intricacies of religious doctrine that had mystified him since his days at the Hollis Street Church. He quickly

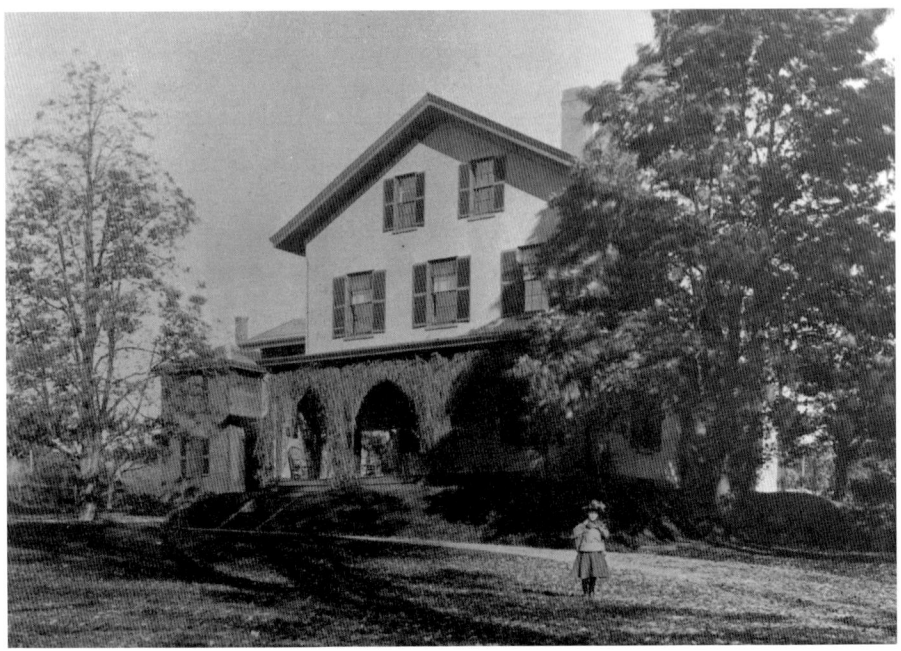

The Pierpont home in West Medford was visited by spirits that discussed weighty matters of theology. *Medford Historical Society.*

paged through his books on spiritualism, learning to his astonishment that his granddaughter was being directly controlled by spirits. If she was developing into a medium, then he had to be sure that she was not being victimized by immortals with evil intentions. This was also the moment to clarify his own perceptions.

In the summer of 1857, Luther Colby was at his desk checking copy for the next edition of the *Banner of Light* when an intense Reverend Pierpont stormed in demanding some answers. The editor mentally reviewed the list of mediums working in Boston. He stopped when he reached the name of James V. Mansfield, the "Spirit Postmaster," whose specialty was answering sealed letters. Intrigued by the concept of a medium corresponding with the beyond, Pierpont memorized the multiple steps in the process. First, he had to write a personal note to a departed acquaintance, seal it securely and mail it to the postmaster. Mansfield would touch the unopened letter while awaiting confirmation from the intended spirit recipient. If communication was established, he would transcribe the immortal's response onto some heavy linen paper. Finally, both items would be shipped back to the client. This decidedly original approach had already gained such momentum that the shelves in Mansfield's office on Winter Street were stacked with thousands of inquiries from all over America and Canada.

Pierpont retired to the silence of his Medford library to compose one of the most important letters of his life. On August 27, he wrote to the spirit of Reverend William Ellery Channing, his mentor and a renowned theologian. Since the minister's passing in 1842, John had believed, or perhaps imagined, that there were many times when William had been present.

The completed document posed a few blunt questions: Was the spirit of Channing contacting him? Did evil spirits use spiritualism to infect and destroy human beings? If spiritualism was God-inspired, what was Pierpont's own role to be in the future of the movement?

He placed the folded paper in a thick folder, which he glued down on all four sides and stamped with his own wax seal as an added precaution. This packet was placed in a larger envelope, along with a request for a response and one dollar plus three stamps to cover expenses. He addressed it to Mr. Mansfield, posting it the next day with some misgivings.

In October, Pierpont picked up his sealed original and a reply written in the medium's penmanship. The news was all good. Addressing him as "My Dear and Beloved Brother Pierpont," the spirit of Channing expressed his support while unequivocally stating that spiritualism was a path to enlightenment that focused on everything good. Evil spirits existed but could be rendered ineffective. Mediums had to be true to their calling, or their own weaknesses would make them unreliable. Channing closed with the promise that he would always be nearby to offer guidance. This personal message was the tipping point that removed doubt and created certainty.

Filled with resolve, Pierpont opened up to a more joyful way of living as well as preaching. In December 1857, he married Harriet Fowler, a forty-six-year-old widow, who dedicated herself to his happiness. Within another year, he was making frequent trips to New York to speak about the God-inspired truths of spiritualism. From time to time, he called on Mr. Mansfield, who had become a friend as well as an adviser. It is more than likely that he witnessed the medium at work, holding a sealed letter in his left hand while taking down dictation from the spirits with his right. He certainly stopped in one evening to get the address of Mrs. Hyde, a medium on Portland Street. One of Pierpont's spirit guides had told him to attend one of her séances because Mary, the spirit of his first wife, was eager to talk about their children and his new life. By the end of the decade, John was placing ads in the *Banner of Light* in which he expressed his eagerness to speak publicly anywhere and to anyone about spiritualism.

Chapter 2
A DEFINITION OF PURPOSE

In 1860, spiritualists were getting ready for change. By the next spring, the world as they knew it would be pulled apart. The events of the Civil War brought Boston believers up against harsh reality on several levels. Many volunteered to fight; some worked for the Federal government. These years were spent looking outward to heal society.

A Year of Being In-Between: 1860

The new decade dawned on a changing and growing Boston. James Wallace Black made an ascent in a hot-air balloon in order to photograph the city from the air, the first image of its kind. New residential land was being created as the filling of the Back Bay reached up to today's Clarendon Street. George Meacham, an architect, was designing the Public Garden as an oasis of horticulture and relaxation. The time was ripe to seize the moment rather than to look back nostalgically. A short editorial in the January 1860 edition of the *Banner* threw out a challenge to Boston spiritualists: "To answer the demands of the age, it is not so necessary to venerate and expound the records of the olden time, as to investigate and to understand the condition of things present, and to adapt our labors to the existing necessities of the world. Those who [look back] may explore the dim labyrinths and incarcerate their souls in the dungeons of the past. In the great light of the Present we live and move, and have our being."

A Definition of Purpose

It was a year to increase knowledge. Formal lectures took center stage every Sunday at the New Melodeon on Washington Street. Dr. Henry Gardner, a key spiritualist organizer, unveiled a meeting place dedicated to knowledge and spiritualism. After months of fundraising, he and his committee were delighted that this splendid hall had become the public face of the movement. Noted speakers were engaged to give fresh insights into classical topics such as the nature of freedom, the cultivation of will power and the potential of personal fulfillment.

Miss Lizzie Doten made history one of the first months that the New Melodeon opened its doors. Her discourse was on St. Paul's provocative statement: "It is a disgrace for women to speak in the church." Much to the surprise of the predominantly male audience, she delivered her lecture with her eyes wide open and her gaze directed at the listeners in front of her. She was entranced—that is, under the influence of her spirit guides—but not passive. This bold posture was a challenge to the traditional view that ladies should always appear nonconfrontational. That evening, Lizzie spoke about the debilitating limits of the "feminine spheres of knowledge." In her opinion, spiritualism was going to free women to use both their hearts *and* minds to enlighten the world. Three years later, she would expand her view. In *Poems from the Inner Life*, a compilation of her verses, she remarked on the power of spirit influence in her own life. Their guidance informed all her intellectual efforts, "like a golden thread" running through a rich fabric.

Along with being receptive to new ideas, believers were urged to practice discernment. The *Banner* recommended that first-time clients of Miss Ada L. Coan, a medium on Tremont Street, "write down the names of deceased friends on billets of paper about three inches square, fold them closely and carry them to her rooms" before attending a séance. This precaution was intended to empower the truth-seeker. Even the mission statement of the Message Department was tightened up to emphasize clear judgment: "We ask the reader to receive no doctrine put forth by spirits in these columns that does not comport with his reason. Each [spirit] expresses so much of the truth as he perceives—no more."

The Bethesda Institute on Tremont Street offered a one-stop assortment of spiritualist experiences in an experiment treating soul, body and mind. Mrs. L.F. Hyde was in attendance to supply private or group séances; Mrs. E.B. Danforth gave business advice while entranced. Medical clairvoyants healed the sick as well as detected the causes of disease. A "Reading Room Resort" was open from 9:00 a.m. to 9:00 p.m. in which music, books on the spiritualist philosophy and comfortable chairs created a nurturing environment. Use of this space was free although donations were welcomed.

It was also the moment for professional mediums to start working on the details of being self-employed. The most problematic area was scheduling. Traditionally, when a client booked a private séance, he expected the session to be extended if the spirits were still communicating. However, he had no intention of paying an additional fee. Clients might also be waiting in the outer room, anxious to begin their appointments. By the spring of 1860, a "Friend to the Cause" was writing to the *Banner* with suggestions on how to "hurry along" séances without compromising quality.

This was the year that more and more believers began to enjoy relaxing together in social activities popular with the middle class. Outings in the country, benefit concerts and community suppers helped to reinforce the bonds shared by the diverse community. One bright Sunday in the heat of July, over three thousand spiritualists traveled by special trains to the town of Reading, north of Boston, for a Grand Mass Picnic at Harmony Grove, where "the fires of love and social fraternity" were kindled again. Coming from Boston, Lowell and Lawrence, participants enjoyed lunch, ice cream and refreshing drinks in the open air before hearing presentations by trance speakers. Mrs. Mary Macumber, a lecturer of limited education who "quaffed deeply from the cup of poverty," was featured because, when entranced, she was eloquent and enlightened in her utterances. These activities drew in other men and women who wanted to know about spiritualism but were not ready to commit themselves.

The Superstar of Spiritualism: Theodore Parker (1810–1860)

The translation into eternity of Reverend Theodore Parker in Italy on May 10, 1860, was a watershed moment for the Boston community. During his earth years, he had been a lightning rod who attracted social activists and repelled the Harvard establishment. A freethinking reformer who was interested in all the major causes of the day, he had preached about spiritualism in the mid-1850s. He was impressed with its focus on democracy and lack of hierarchy. Four years before his death, he wrote down an intriguing thought in his private journal. This movement, he pondered, had the potential to become the most widespread religion in America. Since Parker was committed to freeing the mind from artificial restraints, it was surprising that he never found it necessary to become a spiritualist himself.

A Definition of Purpose

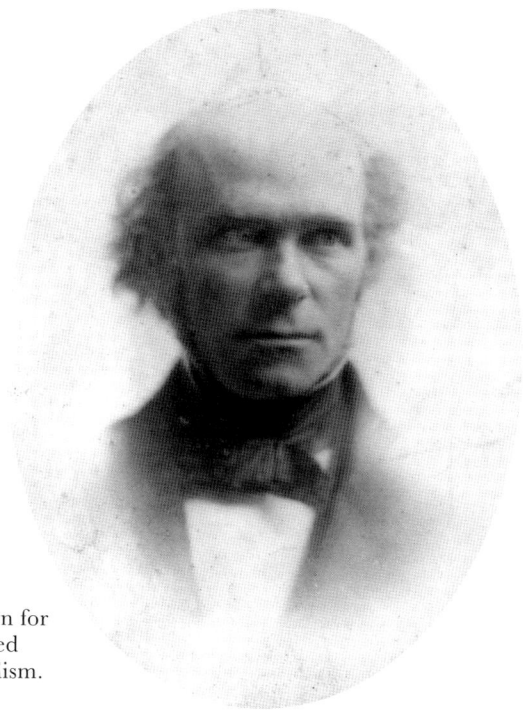

Reverend Theodore Parker, known for his progressive viewpoints, admired the democratic nature of spiritualism. *Author's collection.*

He had an extraordinary ability to reconcile opposites. A fascination with languages was balanced by his love of the soil. His belief in the soul's immortality coexisted with his rejection of Christ's divinity. Because he trusted in a merciful God, he had to reject Calvinistic theology that emphasized human depravity. Even though he was a graduate of the Harvard Divinity School in 1836, he thought that the Bible was awash in contradiction. He loved growing up on a Lexington farm but, like a true son of the Bay State, was not entirely at ease living anywhere other than in or near Boston. His ministry at a church in West Roxbury in the 1840s allowed him enough spare time to extend the hand of fellowship to his neighbors living at Brook Farm, a utopian community. Their exploration of transcendentalism, a philosophy based on self-reliance and the validity of personal intuition, appealed to his passion for independence. On a softer note, he willed all his books to the Boston Public Library in order that the city's residents would have equal access to them.

It was not simply conjecture that Parker was in harmony with the next world. LaRoy Sunderland as far back as 1850 had sensed the presence of spirits making loud raps at the Melodeon Theater and then at the old Music

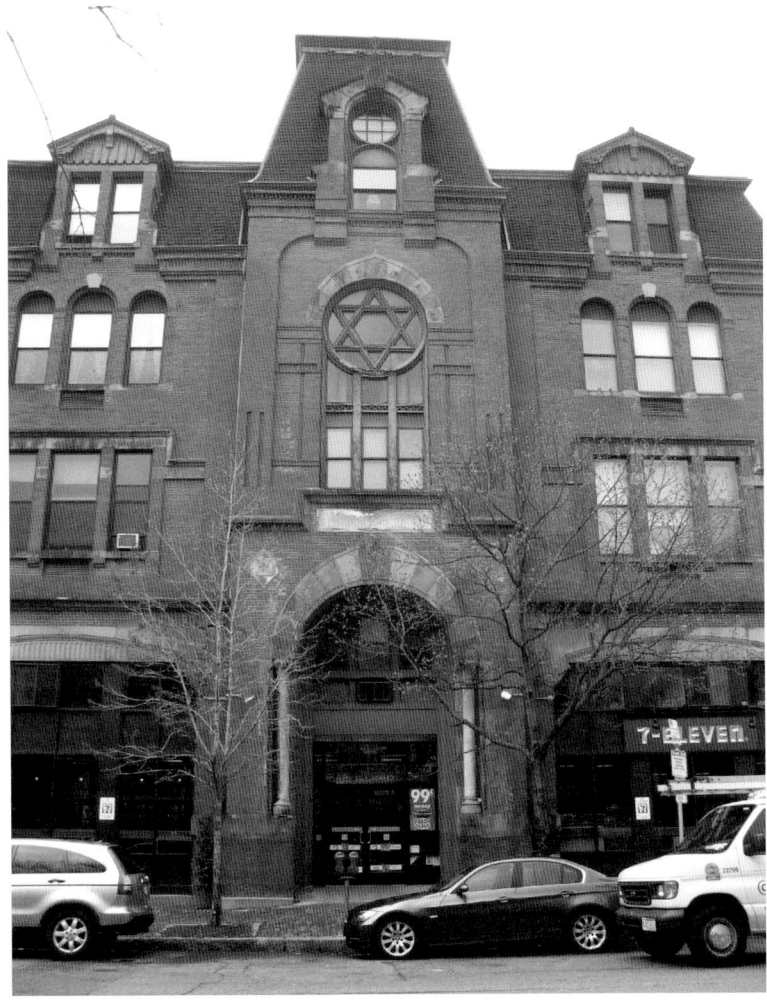

Parker Memorial Hall (1872) in the South End at the corner of Berkeley Street was an important meeting place dedicated to the minister's memory. *Ryan Hayward.*

Hall whenever the reverend preached. The "angels," as LaRoy termed them, burst into a frenzy of staccato beats during sermons on freeing the slaves because Parker could not bear the intrinsic evil in this "peculiar institution." Abolitionism was central to his life and supported by many reform-minded spirits. Other worshipers did not hear the noises, although on occasion, Sunderland reported that the minister looked up quizzically at the chandeliers whenever a particularly loud rap played off the crystal pendants.

Reverend Parker was a much more significant player in the Boston community once he became an immortal. The *Banner* relied on the advice from his spirit to the extent that he was appointed the president-emeritus of the Public Circles, the large public sessions conducted at the *Banner* office by Fanny Conant. As a spirit author, he excelled in outlining and dictating the major events found in the 1873 biography of Mrs. Conant. The narrative of her time on earth was interlaced with personal insights that only he, in his immortal state, would have known. Theodore Parker was the spirit center of Boston spiritualism.

The *Banner* and the Early Conflict

On April 12, 1861, the Confederates fired on Fort Sumter, a Federal fort strategically situated in the entrance to the harbor at Charleston, South Carolina. Although in past years the *Banner* had refused to become embroiled in secular news and debates, Editor Colby now joined other Northerners in expressing his outrage. He and many Boston spiritualists had urged using diplomacy in dealing with the South, but at this time, he wrote, "now we advocate War because that is the only resort left, whereby Peace itself can be assured; because rebels in arms declare that they will govern us and shape our institutions for us or that War shall be our portion; because, while we have stood for peace on their behalf, as much as our own, they have meant only War from the beginning; and because, finally, no single remedy less violent, is less likely to prove efficient in curing the present disease."

The telegraph wires hummed with hourly updates on the attack, but details were lacking. During the assault, a private séance was in progress near the *Banner* office. Luther Colby, the only participant, later wrote about it in the April 27 issue. One of his departed friends, while on earth an executive with an "enterprising, go-ahead disposition," had indicated his presence. The medium, at Colby's urging, asked the spirit to travel to the seat of war in order to report back with as much information as he could gather. The next day, just before noon, Luther and the medium met again in order to receive the immortal's evaluation. The news was disheartening in that the fort was down, and Major Anderson had "got the worst of it" because the soldiers were out of rations and the "laborers just grumbled." A few militants on shore wanted to hold Anderson hostage in order to use him as a negotiating chip with Washington, but spirits friendly to the Federal side protected him.

Charleston residents were so jubilant that some boasted that they would take on New York next. The spirit ended with the prediction that the Southern troops would mobilize in a great and bloody attempt to destroy the North.

The *Banner* patriotically supported the war effort. Colby and other spiritualists frequently walked over to the Common to watch a regiment of one thousand young soldiers performing drills. As the untested troops left Boston for the South, a majority of residents were convinced that the conflict would be brief since the North was better armed and prepared. The inglorious defeat at the first Battle of Bull Run in July, resulting in many deaths and a Union rout, caused one séance attendee to ask for predictions of future victories. He was informed by an adamant immortal that the spirits were aware that the Northern ranks would continue to suffer terribly. Many on both sides, he said, were going to lose their physical bodies; however, the final outcome of the conflict had not been determined.

The Idea of a Regiment of Spiritualists

A tantalizing article appeared in the paper on November 2, 1861. There had been rumors that interested parties were eager to form a regiment of spiritualists. The writer indicated that a well-known medium had already volunteered to command such a select group. This field officer was the grandson of two Revolutionary War heroes and a graduate of a military institution. The lieutenants were "powerful physical mediums, all gentlemen of military experience, good intelligence and courteous bearing." Reverend Mr. Fishbough, a close friend of the iconic Andrew Jackson Davis, had offered to serve as the chaplain, although he was well along in years. Captain Samuel F. Clark, the recruiter, was a Massachusetts clairvoyant, *Banner* correspondent and farmer by profession.

Colby commented that many societies found in orthodox churches were already knitting and sewing for the troops. Spiritualists, he thought, needed to come together to offer similar support. In particular, a group of ladies could create a regimental banner with a beautiful design provided by artists from "the unseen world." The most appealing aspect of the proposal was the knowledge that this "brigade of determined men" would be warriors with no cause to fear death. On November 9, there was a very brief paragraph that indicated that the "plan was in efficient hands" and that readers would be informed as soon as something was known.

Warriors who were clairvoyants and believers! It was a revolutionary concept in 1861. *Author's collection.*

By the end of the month, the *Banner* printed an opinion piece written by A.J. Davis and originally published in the *New York Herald of Progress.* He denounced the suggestion of such a regiment as a step back into sectarianism and the old style of religion. In his opinion, the army should be made up of a cross-section of volunteers representing different denominations, other beliefs or even secular views. What could be more distasteful than creating monolithic military groups composed of all Unitarians or all atheists? "If Spiritualists cannot carry their glorious faith into any Regiment, and be sustained by it, they are not up to their own noble standards," wrote Davis in a strongly worded commentary published in the *Banner.* After the war, Emma Hardinge, an English medium, noted that this unique regiment remained just an idea. She had reviewed correspondence that documented events when soldiers who were spiritualists had effectively advised their commanding officers during battles. Unfortunately, she chose not to name names even though "numerous cases had been recorded."

The Public Circles Connect

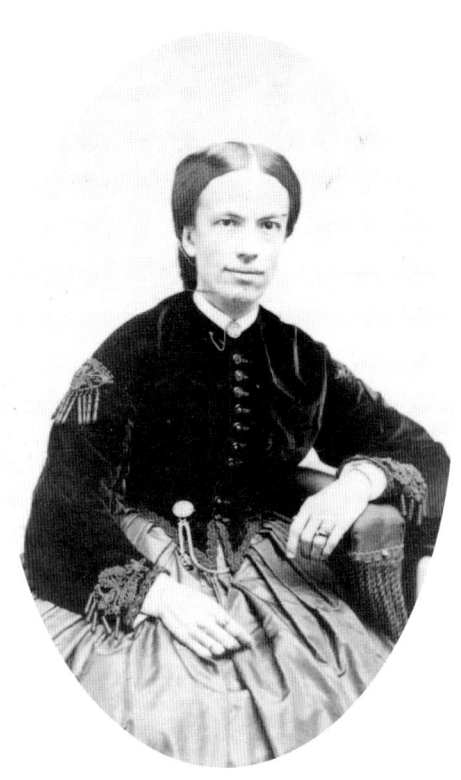

Fanny Conant, the highly respected medium of the *Banner*, devoted herself to delivering spirit messages to Boston audiences. *Author's collection.*

During these increasingly stressful days, the Public Circles, the enormously popular open meetings held at the *Banner* building, were visited by spirits with dramatically contrasting opinions. On April 24, 1861, the spirit of John Brown, the fiery abolitionist executed in 1859, felt compelled to speak through Mrs. Conant, the primary medium on staff. He stated that he no longer blamed God for allowing him to die. Though still getting used to existence as a spirit, he had been inspired to acknowledge that "there are many left on earth so like myself that, through them, I can work effectively." During the same session, the spirit of James Burns, an uneducated laborer from South Boston, criticized Brown, whom he described as "that old fellow who talks about being helped by God." Burns thought that Brown was much more likely to be under the power of the devil than of any supreme being. He had been informed that his two sons had joined the Union army against his wishes. In his heart, the Irish spirit did not think that blacks were worth fighting for.

The Circles now took place three times a week in spacious rooms decorated with portraits of living spiritualists and sketches done by spirit-artists who created their work by controlling the brushes and pens of receptive mediums. Fanny mounted a raised platform in the center of the chamber while a *Banner* employee locked the outer doors. She became entranced under the guidance of Theodore Parker, the ultimate spirit guide. An invocation to the "Supreme Intelligence" was offered. After settling any current questions, Mrs. Conant introduced the spirits who were seeking out the physical world.

A Definition of Purpose

Any Circle might host teenagers, a Native American, a Catholic widow or tradesmen from the past. During the war, soldiers from both sides made their presence known, often with accents intact.

The War Takes a Life in 1862

Spirits had twice warned William Berry, Colby's intense co-editor, not to throw his life away. The first occurred during the 1850s, when Fanny Conant was holding a séance at his North Cambridge home. Dr. John Dix Fisher, her spirit guide, asked her to deliver the dire message that William would perish on a battlefield sometime in the future. Learning to rein in his impulsive nature and become more practical in his decisions was the only way to prevent this from happening. Fisher then summoned a very combative spirit who had been killed during the Mexican-American War of 1846. When the being touched Fanny, the deafening roar of invisible cannons mixed with the rapid retort of unseen rifles immediately filled the parlor. Berry and everyone in the audience covered their ears to block out the noise of deadly conflict. After this event, Fanny asked her host if he had received any important insights. Berry shrugged.

The second attempt was made by a warlike spirit named Captain Gibbs, who had once been a pirate on the

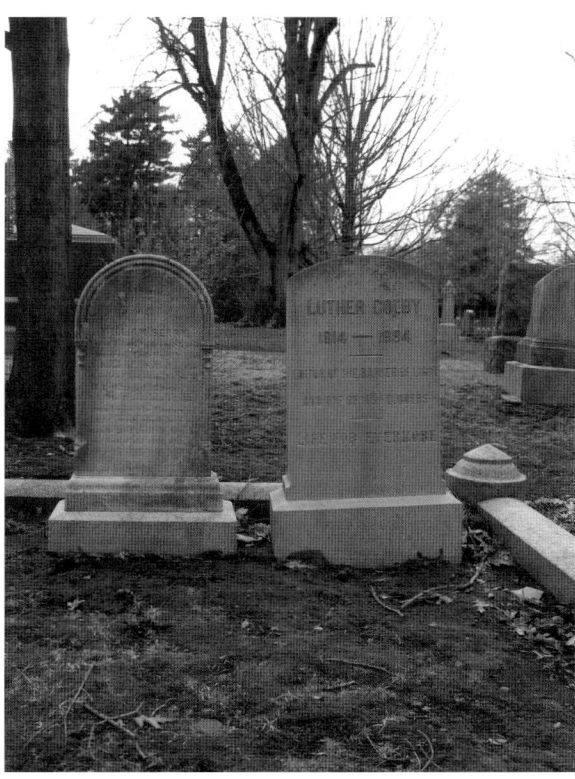

William Berry (left) and Luther Colby (right) were colleagues in life. They are still side by side at Forest Hills. *Ryan Hayward.*

high seas. Possessing some psychic ability of his own, Berry was unruffled when this invisible spirit worked with him on projects related to the *Banner*. Their telepathic conversations became testy, however, when Gibbs got more personal and announced that they would soon be "shaking hands on the spirit side of life" unless William modified his rash temperament. Again, Berry disregarded the advice.

William could not wait to volunteer for service in 1861. By mid-August, he was training with the First Company of Andrew Sharpshooters attached to the Fifteenth Regiment of Massachusetts. He was a cocky sergeant of thirty-six summers, proud to be more seasoned than many of his men. By early 1862, Berry had been promoted to full first lieutenant and was sending home exciting descriptions of combat. Colby would later comment that his friend was "constitutionally blind to all sense of danger." It certainly seemed that he was under the protection of spirits because bullets struck trees near him, yet he was left unscathed.

At two o'clock on the morning of September 17, Officer Berry wrote his final letter. He mentioned that preparations were being made to engage in a great battle and that his mind was racing in anticipation. Little did he realize that the spirit messages from years past were about to come true. The two sides clashed violently near Sharpsburg, Maryland, close to the banks of the Antietam Creek. After attacks and counterattacks coupled with poor decisions on the part of the Union's overly cautious General McClellan, a Federal victory was declared despite the slaughter. The battlefield was drenched with the blood of many wounded and dying soldiers. Toward the top of a rise, Lieutenant Berry lay fatally shot. He had rushed to take the place of his fallen commanding officer in a gallant, impetuous effort to lead his fellow soldiers to victory. At least one of his men had cautioned him to be more prudent.

Colby wrote his colleague's obituary in the first week of October, filled with "poignant grief" as he paid his respects to a "stouthearted soldier" who had made the ultimate sacrifice. He praised William's devotion to the *Banner*, as well as his sterling qualities. Berry had died for a noble cause during his earthly existence but was very much alive in the next world. The *Banner* of October 4, 1862, said, "His death is but the evidence of his change of position, he having departed to the other side where he can still prosecute his work with all his soul and strength. His life—like all our lives—was a struggle, sometimes a strife, but in his death he became immortal indeed."

As the years moved on, the spirit of Berry continued to promote the *Banner* by appearing frequently at the Pubic Circles. Mrs. Conant felt

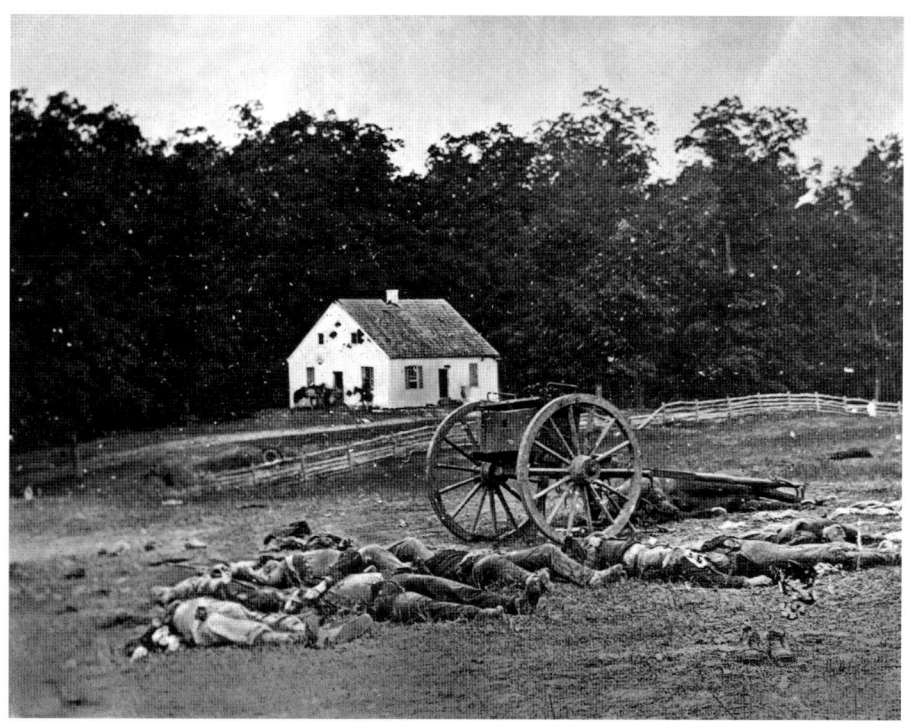

William Berry was fatally wounded at the Battle of Antietam in September 1862. *Corbis Images.*

that eternity had softened his personality, but he never admitted to her whether he had shaken hands with his spirit guide, the swashbuckling Captain Gibbs.

THE MINDSET OF THE EDITOR, 1863–65

In 1863, Colby worried that because the state of American civilization was hopelessly "deep in blood-streams and begrimed with powder stains," there was not enough energy to accomplish the monumental task at hand. Yet he soon rallied to support the Emancipation Proclamation, which he called the "greatest step in progress of the nineteenth century; its results will be mighty for good not only to the North, but the South also, in the coming time." He had justifiable pride in the number of *Banner* compositors, printers and clerks who volunteered and made sure to mention F. Frank White, a popular trance lecturer, who served as a lieutenant in the adventuresome United States Balloon Corps. He also praised Oliver C. Cooper, an administrator in the office, who was one of half a dozen on the staff who enlisted as privates. And he grieved with his *Banner* colleague from New York, S. Brittan, whose son was killed in a naval battle. A.E. Newton, the frequent columnist, volunteered to work for the Freedman's Bureau, helping to set up schools in the South and later in the capital. John Pierpont worked in the Treasury Department. In their free time, both men spread the news of spiritualism through public lectures.

Somehow the editor kept alive his conviction that the war was going to end soon, but that belief was difficult to sustain on the day he walked to the Common to help welcome home a regiment of battle-weary soldiers. The men had been sent to Boston for a month while more volunteers were recruited. It was an occasion to celebrate their return, but at the same time, this was so unlike the festive send-off that he had witnessed two years previously. He then encouraged a major reorganization within the army in order that the next "season" of battles would be decisive enough to "end the rebellion and bring peace to our country." Part of his responsibility, he often wrote, was to remind the public that negative thinking would seriously undermine the cause just when victory was on the horizon.

He tried to strike a balance in his 1864 editorials by acknowledging that the war years had robbed too many households of their dearest and most honored husbands, fathers and brothers. Then he always moved to his core belief that as much as the memories were sacred treasures, there was the eternal reality that had to remain in the forefront. These valiant spirits were alive and within reach. It was not surprising that the Public Circles, gaining more and more attention as the war progressed, had frequent visits from the spirits of different ranks of soldiers, even Confederates who were not sure that they would be welcomed. Mrs. Conant received them all graciously.

On April 3, 1865, Colby was almost unable to contain his joy when the Rebel capital fell. He was ecstatic that African American soldiers were some of the first to enter Richmond, where they discovered that the Confederate leaders had deserted their posts. "That fact alone," he commented, "seemed to have a strong tinge of poetic justice in it!" The assassination of President Lincoln a few days later filled him with despair at the loss of a leader who had preserved the Union despite many setbacks. There was still much to accomplish. He wrote, "We have been repeatedly told by our angel-guides that these latter days were to subject us to trials the likes of which we had never seen before; that old things would be changed, and old systems broken up, and the result of all would be a thorough schooling in humility, patience and faith."

Colby concluded his piece by putting his faith in an all-knowing and merciful God and the spirit guides that had pledged to carry out the Divine Plan.

The Unflappable Healer: Charles H. Crowell (1828–1869)

During this decade of turmoil, it was significant that Colby had the assistance of Charles H. Crowell, Fanny Conant's older brother. This carpenter by trade had first worked at the Watertown Arsenal for Major Wainwright, a dedicated spiritualist. Charles was soon convinced that he was communicating with spirits. By 1860, he had switched careers to become a magnetic healer, with the *Banner* attesting to his honesty, as well as his psychic ability to diagnose ailments. His rooms in the newspaper's office building were always busy with clients seeking medicinal compounds prepared under the supervision of reliable physicians in the spiritual realm. His particular spirit guide, Dr. Rufus Kittredge, was such an influence that Charles chose to name his firstborn son after the deceased country doctor.

In contrast to his friend, the mercurial William Berry, Crowell was a study in calm reliability. Luther Colby depended on him to substitute, on short notice, for any lecturer who neglected to fulfill an engagement. He could be counted on to represent the *Banner*'s interests at every convention, no matter how inconvenient the timing. Undemanding and self-abnegating, he returned to his job the day after he came home from his nine months of service in the Massachusetts Eleventh Battery.

His belief in the spirit world was severely tested in 1865 when two of his children succumbed to diphtheria, a respiratory disease common in Victorian times. After the sudden transition of Eva, his six-year-old, Charles looked to his sister for consolation at the close of the business day at the *Banner* office. Mrs. Conant observed a spirit hand remove a white flower from a vase and offer it to her brother. This appeared to be a foreshadowing of a second death within the family. Three days later, young Fannie, named in her honor, passed to the other world, having caught a fatal infection from Eva.

The funeral, as later reported in the *Banner*, was unusual even for devoted believers. As Charles stood by the casket, he noticed a spirit child approach.

She touched his hand and asked, "Is that me? Am I a spirit?" Without hesitating, her father let her pat the cheek of her own mortal remains. He was grief-stricken yet consoled when the apparition faded from sight. Just then, the choir sang "Shall We Know Each Other Over There?" All this transpired in full view of the mourners who, except for Mrs. Conant and another medium, were unaware that anything extraordinary had taken place.

The Watertown Lodge and Native American Spirits

Even the stoic Mr. Crowell needed to relax in a peaceful environment. Charles; his wife, Julia; their remaining children; and Fanny Conant moved to the leafy suburb of Watertown in 1866. The house had been given the name Kanagawah Lodge, which meant "teacher." This honor was bestowed by Native American spirits in recognition of the mediums' active support of this struggling race. To return the compliment, Fanny filled the walls of the séance room with portraits of tribal chiefs and medicine men. Her enthusiasm was doubled when Theodore Parker's spirit informed her that some of her ancestors had been Native American seers.

From her very early days as a practicing medium, Mrs. Conant had a particular fondness for communicating with beings that were imbued with respect for the earth's healing powers. She relied on their energy to sustain her during long sessions at the Public Circles. Often, while entranced, she would lapse into a variety of dialects that were meaningless to her when she was conscious. One client, an agent for the United States Indian Bureau, confirmed that she was speaking in the Sioux tongue when Spring Flower, a spirit child from that tribe, was present.

The Cheyenne Protege: Minnie Tappan or Em-Mu-Ne-Es-Ka (1857–1873)

A very endearing example of cross-cultural bonding existed between Fanny and Minnie Tappan, the daughter of a Cheyenne chief. When the Second Colorado Cavalry, under the command of Lieutenant Colonel Chivington, engaged in a cold-blooded massacre of the men, women and children of

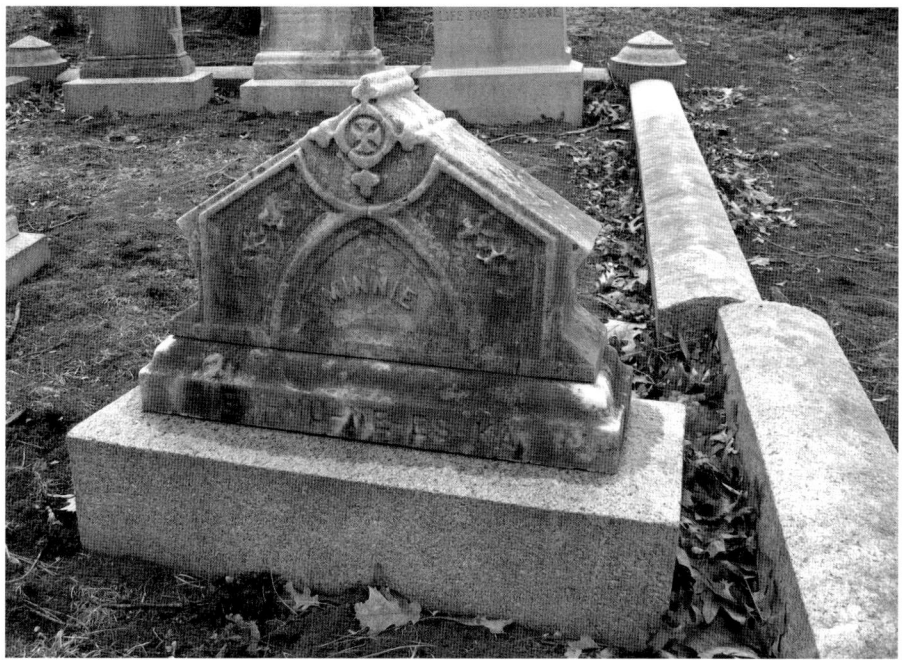

Minnie Tappan was the Cheyenne protégé of Fanny Conant. Her monument displays her Native American name. *Ryan Hayward.*

a peaceful village in the Colorado Territory, there were few survivors. On November 29, 1864, Minnie escaped the carnage by remaining hidden. She was rescued and sent to an Indian Mission School, where Colonel S.F. Tappan was drawn to her. He adopted the child, gave her his name and returned east. During her eighteen months in Boston, she became the protégé of Fanny Conant, who sent her to the public schools. Minnie responded well to her surroundings and was found to possess clairvoyant powers. It came time for her to study at Howard University in preparation to become a teacher. Consumption took hold, and she "gradually passed from the form" on November 23, 1873.

Her funeral rites were celebrated in Boston at the home of a spiritualist who was friendly with Colonel Tappan. Fanny set aside a place in her lot at Forest Hills Cemetery as a suitable burial site. Mrs. Conant performed a Native American ritual taught to her by her spirit guides. This included beating a drum and placing Indian corn on the soil as a symbol of the land of plenty to which the Cheyenne spirit was going. At the request of the invisibles, Fanny scattered triangles of white paper containing messages for

Minnie to carry into eternity. Within days, the spirit of Minnie had visited the Public Circles to assure "Aunt Fanny" that she had entered the spirit land of her forefathers.

The Musical Medium: Annie Lord Chamberlain

Mrs. Chamberlain, a fresh-faced twenty-year-old with no bad habits, nice features and a cheerful expression, became a rising star in the 1860s Boston firmament. F.G. Keith, a satisfied client, summed up the public's generous acceptance of her performance art. He approved Colby's request to print his testimonial on March 3, 1862: "Let skeptics visit Mrs. Chamberlain's circles, honorably observe the conditions, and if they can account for the phenomena on other grounds than those claimed, we shall certainly be pleased to hear them."

One of her first séances took place at the home of Mr. Lane in South Malden, a middle-class city north of Boston. Two dozen spiritualists assembled, including Charles Crowell from the *Banner* office. Mrs. Lane was delighted to host such an exceptional event. In the large square parlor, there was a small table with a full array of instruments, starting with a guitar, violincello and tambourine and ending with a collection of bells, some without clappers. A large bass drum was securely fastened to the wall near the display. Mixed in with the instruments was a bow and arrow set, plus a small water flask. Pieces of red sugar candy were scattered about.

Mrs. Chamberlain entered and, after exchanging a few pleasantries with the guests, took her place at the end of a large black walnut dining table, where she sat with her back to the props. She then arranged the guests, alternating male and female, and asked that they join hands. After the singing of a familiar song by the audience, the energy level in the room was increased. Then the kerosene light was extinguished at the request of the spirits. The people on either side of the medium anchored down her dress with their chair legs in order that she could not move around. At once, there was the sound of the guitar being strummed as it seemed to rise unaided into the air and pass over the heads of the participants. The violin was somehow tossed onto the large table as the animated guitar put forth a gentle tune before thumping down beside it. In rapid succession, various bells rang out, and the bass drum contributed an occasional low boom. Charles Crowell asked in a loud whisper to be recognized by the spirits. Within seconds, a

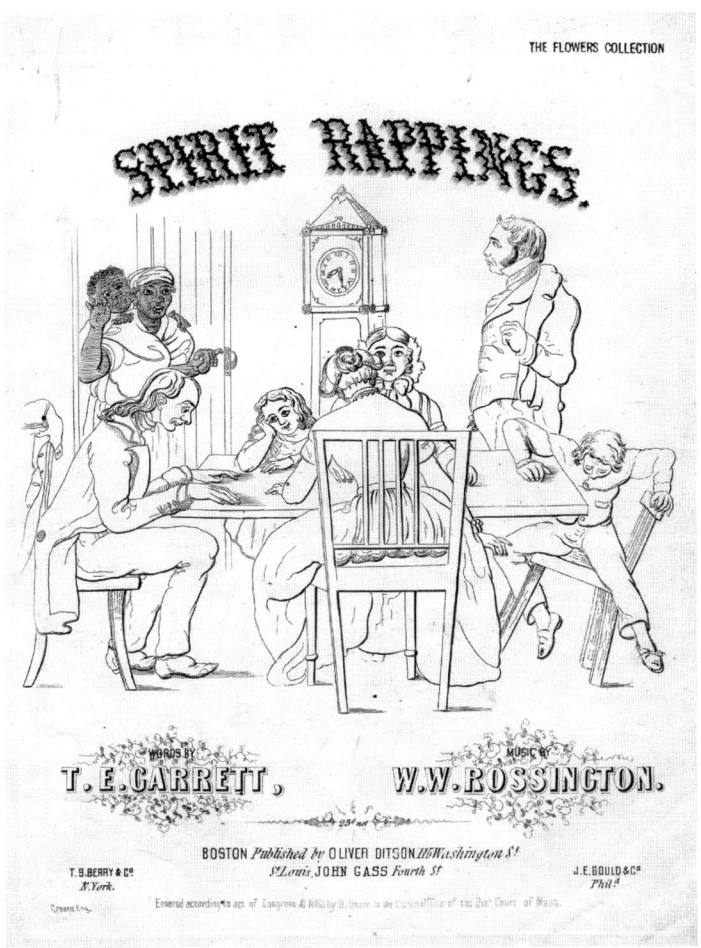

"Spirit Rappings" sheet music provided a more informal and popular look at the movement of spiritualism. *Historical American Sheet Music Collection, David M. Rubenstein Rare Book and Manuscript Library, Duke University.*

bell was dropped into his lap, and then more and more items piled up until the fifteen pieces started slipping to the rug. A soft, cool hand tugged at his whiskers. The show-off guitar rose up, produced a folk tune and then deposited itself onto the wide expanse of a portly woman's dress. While the bow and arrow danced with the bells, pieces of candy were balanced on participants' heads. Everyone was enjoying the impromptu performances.

Sensing Mrs. Chamberlain's fatigue, the host announced that the spirits were leaving in deference to her exhaustion and the fact that the room energy was decreasing. The light was restored while Annie was escorted to a side parlor, where she was obliged to rest for an hour. Charles Crowell quickly returned to Boston, where he filed an enthusiastic report. He had the "utmost confidence in the medium's honesty." Colby also pronounced Mrs. Chamberlain "a lady whom we cheerfully recommend to the skeptical public."

Annie continued to receive excellent reviews on her way up the popularity ladder. John S. Adams of the Clairvoyant Institute put his twelve years of experience on the line by proclaiming her to be "astonishing." He was accustomed to dealing with temperamental psychics, so her cheerful personality was a refreshing change.

An unexpected endorsement was written by an officer on leave from the Fifty-fifth Massachusetts Regulars. He was impressed that Mrs. Chamberlain had asked the spirits to show him proof of their compassion during his visit to Charlestown in August. The touch of spirit hands reminded him in a melancholy but tender way of his wife, who had died just months before. He was captivated by the melodies of the suspended guitar and sprightly ringing of the bells. But most of all, he was emotionally refreshed when unseen beings sprinkled him with water after everyone sang "The Morning Light Is Breaking." His visit to the séance gave him such a sense of renewal that he thought he was feeling the grace of baptism.

By the end of the year, Annie was invited to have her own Circle Room at the *Banner* office, where her instruments floated, gave forth upbeat music and pleased audiences, who looked forward to having their faces caressed. Her new sessions featured primitive-looking drums that were played by Native American spirits able to manipulate the instruments with extraordinary precision. A violinist hired for the occasion often sat outside the circle and furnished some tunes that guided the beats. When the suite was illuminated again, all the drums, along with the usual guitars, were piled topsy-turvy in the center of the table. The very loud clash of sounds in addition to the disarray of the room proved that Annie's manifestations were completely legitimate. Since she had remained in her chair, kept in physical contact with the customers and had interjected occasional comments, there was a consensus that she could not be the source of the music.

Mrs. Chamberlain was a welcome respite from the uncertainty that seemed constantly present during the Civil War. Her séances did not provide advice or information. Instead, she offered a nonjudgmental bridge between the strife-torn existence of daily life and the tranquility of eternity. After a successful outing to West Roxbury, Annie was honored to have another medium who attended the séance leave a message that was relayed in the July 16, 1864 *Banner*: "What you have seen tonight is but the prelude of that which is to come. The time is rapidly approaching when the two worlds [of earth and spirit] will be so assimilated that their inhabitants will see eye to eye."

A Definition of Purpose

Companion Animals Find Eternity: Carlo (1852–1870)

Boston spiritualists were interested in a number of reform movements during their pursuit of an enlightened earthly life leading into the hereafter. Humane treatment of animals was another cause that was gaining serious attention at the time. It resonated with Fanny Conant, the premier medium of the *Banner*, who was well aware of the circumstances that brought about the Massachusetts Society for the Prevention of Cruelty to Animals.

George Thorndike Angell, the founder of the organization, was a lawyer already committed to defending the defenseless given his partnership with Samuel Sewell, a staunch abolitionist. In 1868, Angell witnessed the outcome of a forty-mile horse race that ended with the two equine rivals collapsing and then dying on the streets of Boston. He was moved to write a public letter expressing his outrage. A number of Beacon Hill women added their social clout, and within weeks, the new animal-oriented society was incorporated. The *Banner* and other progressive journals promoted the organization's fundraising fairs and reported on the successful prosecution of acts of cruelty committed against workhorses.

Mrs. Conant gradually came to a more profound, if not extreme, position. She believed that companion animals deserved an existence beyond their years serving mankind. When she questioned her guides, they agreed. Her proof rested on the story of Carlo, her faithful canine companion for almost two decades.

Fanny had devoted herself to the *Banner of Light* since the early days of 1857, yet her delicate constitution demanded some down time for rest and sleep. Her long hours as the medium of the Public Circles drained her emotionally. Retreating to her rented rooms after completing an afternoon at the *Banner* office, she sought out the company of Carlo, a very ordinary-looking dog with a smooth brindle coat, erect ears and a short tail. He had been her constant companion through all the years she had been her husband's caretaker.

As demands on her time and skills increased, she feared that undeveloped spirits were following her home from the newspaper office. Their agitation filled her with the undeniable dread that they would do her harm. Carlo always stayed by her side as she paced the floor for hours. She understood that his menacing growls were directed toward the ghostly beings that darted about the apartment. Even when commanded to lie down, the usually obedient pet insisted on snapping at the intruders. Carlo would finally leap

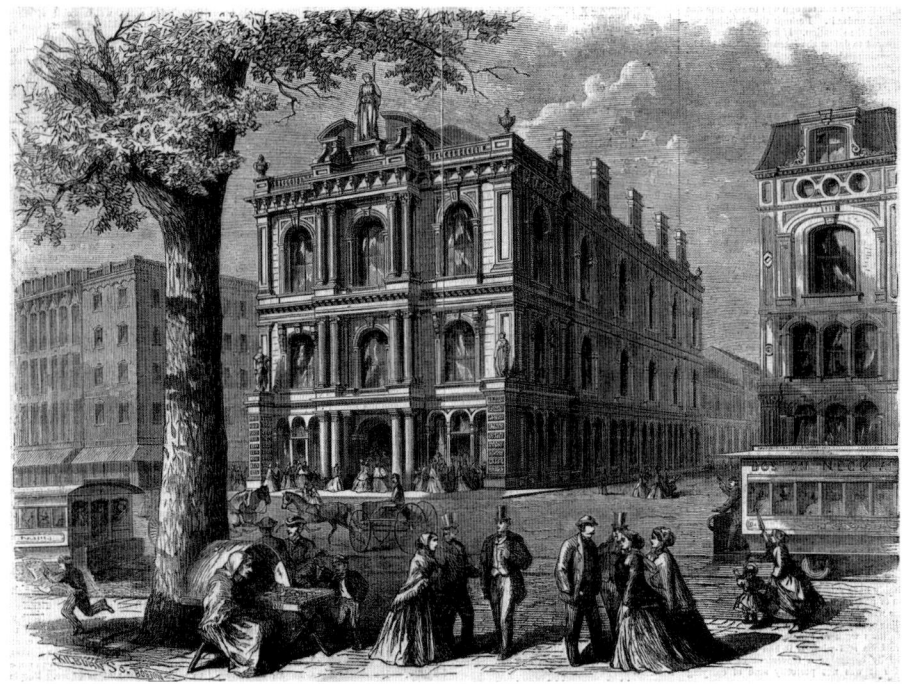

Charles Crowell's funeral at Horticultural Hall in 1869 was a celebration of a life dedicated to truth. *Author's collection.*

joyously about when he sensed that he had chased the malicious spirits back to their origins.

On another occasion while doing errands, Fanny was overcome with a debilitating weakness brought on by her chronic heart condition. Fortunately, she was near the office of Dr. Pike, her longtime physician. He was able to transport her home, even carrying her up the stairs to her rooms. Once inside, the physician saw Carlo spring up, throw his body against Fanny and start to lick her face in earnest. Dr. Pike's first thought was to drive the dog away; however, his own spirit guides counseled him not to. Fanny, upon regaining consciousness, said that her dog's sudden blow to her chest must have restarted her heart.

Fanny reached a fuller appreciation of Carlo when she was confronted with a deeply distressed client who had scheduled a private sitting. The woman was so inconsolable that she could barely speak, leaving the medium to seek answers by becoming entranced. She had a vision of a parrot with red and blue plumage perched in a large palm tree. When restored to herself,

Fanny was informed that the lady's pet of many years had recently died. The bird, a large multi-colored parrot, had made her solitude bearable after the passing of her husband. Fanny reassured her that the spirits were sending a clear message. Any bond that strong would not be broken.

During his senior years, Carlo and his mistress boarded with Mrs. DeWitt, a close spiritualist friend who owned a dog named Gip. The two pets developed an understanding whereby the young terrier shared his food bowl and sleeping mats while the eighteen-year-old respected the youngster's treats. Often the small canine would be seen grabbing onto Carlo's collar as he guided his elderly companion through the crowded streets of the North End.

On Christmas Day 1870, Carlo succumbed to old age. Fanny placed him in his bed and then buried him in the plot that she owned at Forest Hills Cemetery. The next morning, she was favored with a vision of her brother, whose mortal remains had been interred there several months before. As he spoke about the beauties of eternity, Charles's hand rested gently on the head of a spirit dog, whose rejuvenated body was pressed to his side. Carlo had transitioned successfully.

Chapter 3
THE REJECTION OF BOUNDARIES

Boston's physical footprint was enlarged tremendously during this decade by the annexation of six formerly independent neighborhoods. West Roxbury, Jamaica Plain and heavily populated Dorcester are located to the south and Allston and Brighton are situated toward the west, while Charlestown is just across the river. The *Boston Globe*, a new daily, introduced a different perspective. The Great Fire of 1872 changed the appearance of forty acres of the city.

A Phoenix Rises from the Ashes: The Boston Fire of 1872

At 7:00 p.m. on Saturday, November 9, 1872, a red glare lit up the sky at the corner of Summer and Kingston Streets. One of the largest stone mercantile buildings in the heart of the city was engulfed in flames. Boxes of dry goods in the cellar, bolts of fabric on the counters of first-floor shops and trimmings in the sewing girls' workrooms provided the fuel. Mansard roofs, with their steep sides, capped most of the structures, trapping the fire inside the attic floors. The two-day inferno wiped away forty acres of prime real estate defined by Summer, Washington and Milk Streets. Set squarely in the path of the blaze, the bookstore and office of the *Banner of Light* on Washington Street were obliterated.

THE REJECTION OF BOUNDARIES

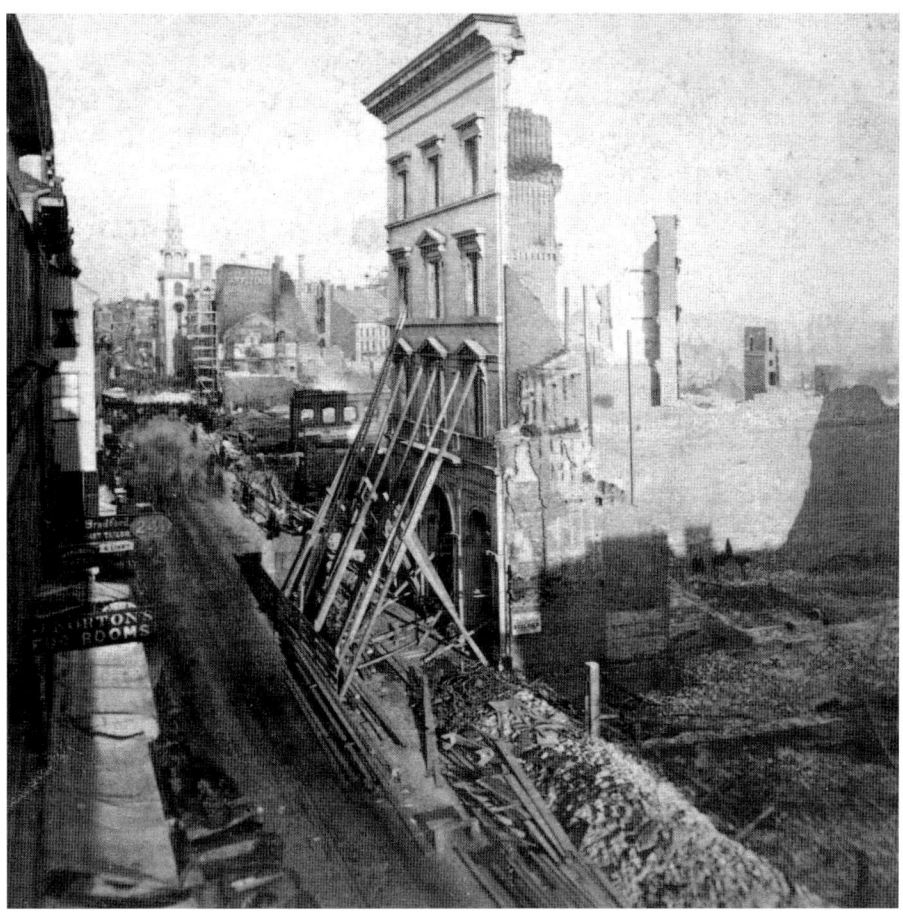

After the Fire of 1872, Washington Street was a charred tableau of ruined buildings. The *Banner* lost everything in the blaze. *Ryan Hayward.*

Fire horses had been out of service for days because many were suffering from a hoof disease. Obliged to pull the wagons themselves, firemen were delayed in coming to the scene, only to discover that their hoses were too short to send a water stream to the top floors. The flames were finally conquered after major efforts were expended by fire companies from Boston and surrounding towns. What remained almost defied description. An eyewitness, Charles Coffin Carleton, documented his impressions in his book about the Great Fire: "The streets of the burned district are so filled with granite, marble and brick, piled in chaotic confusion, and there is such a wilderness of broken walls and chimneys, that we have been lost amid the ruins."

Everything of value, except for some printing plates, was in a charred pile of debris. The room for the Public Circles, plus all the retail stock and correspondence, existed in memory alone. Without wasting time wringing their hands, Colby and the staff found a second-floor space on Hanover Street in which to function. December 14 marked the publishing of the first post-fire paper, set in brand-new type. Subscribers were particularly generous in donating funds to help pay for all the new equipment and supplies. At one of the first Public Circles held at the temporary quarters in Fraternity Hall, Fanny greeted the spirit of James Tibbetts, a Boston fireman who had died in the blaze. He had come to reassure everyone that the *Banner* would rise like a phoenix from the ashes. By October 1873, Colby had secured rooms on Montgomery Place at the corner of Province Street. The effort to sustain the paper was formidable and could not have happened without the support of the readers.

Too Good to Be True: William H. Mumler (1832–1884)

The business of spirit photography began in the 1860s. About 1861, William H. Mumler was reputed to be one of the most skilled ornamental engravers in the city. He worked for the exclusive jewelry firm of Bigelow Brothers and Kennard, where for twenty years he had been entrusted with personalizing valuables owned by the socially prominent. Growing up on Hanover Street in the North End, he had achieved a level of expertise well beyond that of his co-workers. The five to eight dollars that he was paid each day, a handsome sum in the early 1860s, provided enough extra cash to squander a bit on his latest interest. Many times a month, Mumler hurried to Mrs. Stuart's photographic gallery on Washington Street, where a friend processed the glass plates that served as negatives. Mumler was so omnipresent that Mrs. Stuart eventually allowed him to experiment with some of the chemicals as long as he was carefully supervised. It was always breathtaking to watch a finely detailed portrait develop on the treated surface within a few minutes.

One Sunday, Mumler entered the shop building to spend some quality time with his comrade and discovered, to his amazement, that he was entirely alone in the studio. He had often imagined this golden opportunity. William recited the photographic process aloud as he first prepared a plate, which he then inserted into the bulky camera. After removing the lens cap,

The Rejection of Boundaries

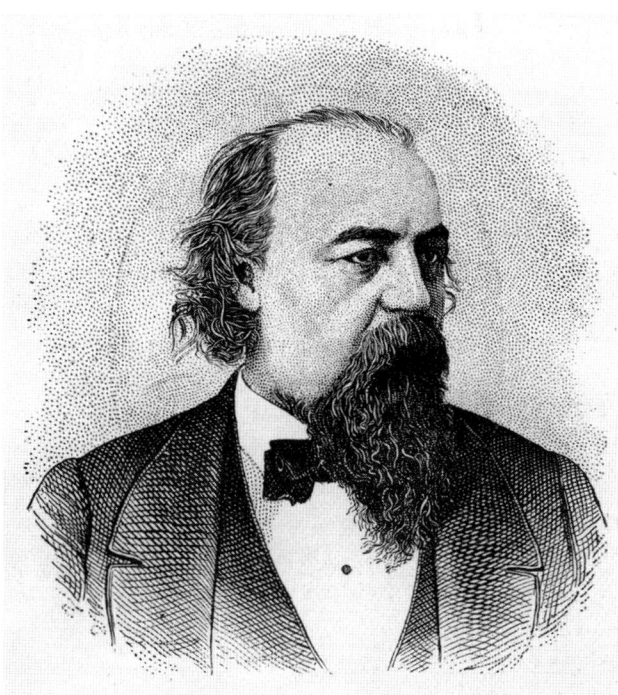

William H. Mumler produced spirit-photographs that contained the semi-transparent image of a departed loved one. *Boston Public Library.*

he self-consciously struck a pose in which he stood with one hand on a chair and the other holding the black drape that he had just removed from the equipment. Then, carefully carrying the exposed glass into the dark room, he prayed that he would finish the procedure correctly. His solo effort began well as he observed his self-portrait taking shape; however, his confidence suddenly plummeted. He saw a second form that was transparent, ethereal and oddly familiar. A ghostly young girl was awkwardly seated in the chair, surrounded with wisps of cloudy vapors. Mumler's first reaction was that she looked like a cousin who had died over twelve years ago. Could this be a spirit image? He was aware of the concepts of spiritualism but had not wanted to explore them. During the next week, he showed the anomaly to Mrs. Stuart's assistant, who diagnosed the double picture as the result of residue left from an improperly cleaned glass negative. That was the most logical explanation.

Mumler printed a copy to display at the jewelry store for the amusement of his customers and friends. When one client, a spiritualist, asked for more information, William joked that the photograph was taken when he was the only living person in the studio. The man requested that the engraver write that statement on the back of the card along with the date and his signature. Having handed it over as a souvenir, Mumler never anticipated that he would be the subject of any publicity.

Weeks later, he was dismayed to read an article about the photograph in the *Banner of Light*. The story had first been printed in the *Herald of Progress*, a New York paper published by famous psychic Andrew J. Davis and then picked up by the Boston sheet as an item of local interest. It even indicated the address of the gallery. He rushed over to the Washington Street studio to apologize for his lapse in judgment.

The reception room was filled with men and women asking about the new process. A young lady named Hannah, the future Mrs. Mumler, called out from behind the sales counter, "Here comes the spirit photographer!" One gentleman demanded an immediate appointment despite William's protests that he was not a professional. After getting the nod from Mrs. Stuart, Mumler filled the request by taking multiple images. When he developed the fourth attempt, he was more surprised than his sitter to see a spirit form appear on the negative. Of course, the news spread quickly that the departed were receptive to being photographed. Mumler himself was repeatedly questioned by Bostonians eager to submit themselves to the experiment. As more and more customers contacted him, William was obliged to quit the engraving business in order to work full time for Mrs. Stuart. Luther Colby of the *Banner* was excited but urged caution. In November 1862, he wrote, "We have been assured for months by our spirit-friends that in due time the mundane world would be startled by this new phase of spirit power; but we were not prepared to receive it so soon, and are yet in doubt that the manifestation is entirely legitimate."

Taking those words seriously, several local spiritualists, such as the respected Dr. Henry Gardner, gathered eyewitness testimony. Mr. Plummer, one of Mrs. Stuart's employees, reported that he often worked in the same room where Mumler held his sittings, using the same camera when his turn came. They frequently worked together to develop the plates. If there was deception, it was beyond his knowledge. One of the veteran Boston photographers was asked to imitate William's work if he could. He complied but declared that he needed two negatives to get the same effect that Mumler achieved with only one. A.J. Davis sent his own investigator, photographer William Guay, who was convinced that it was impossible for Mumler to counterfeit the spirit representations. Mr. Edson, a trusted observer, summed up their weeks of due diligence when he addressed the Boston Spiritualist Conference in November 1862: "If [spirit-photography] is true, it will in

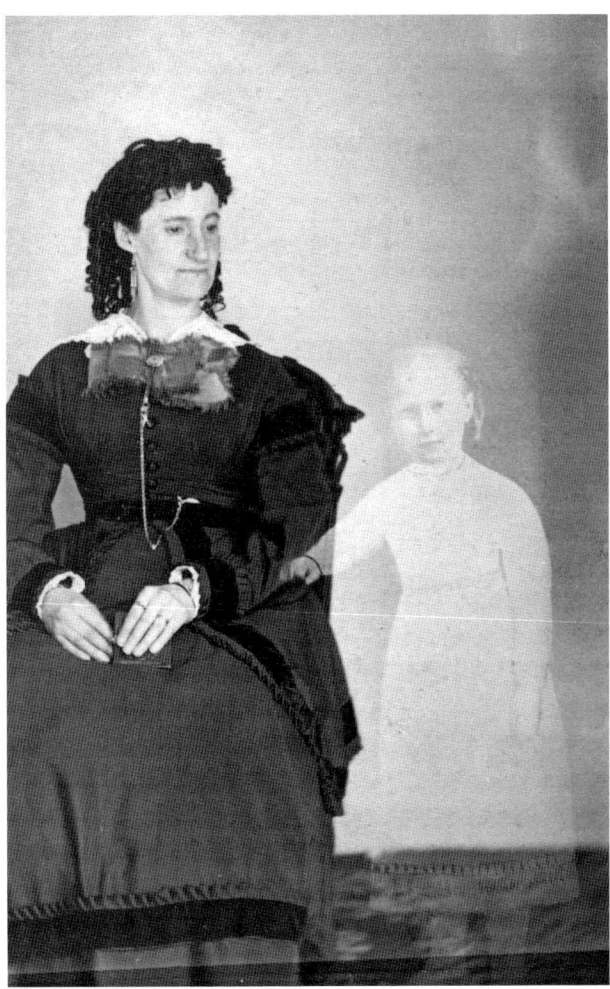

Mrs. Tinkman was delighted to see the form of this spirit-child. It was visible proof that the little one was in eternity. *Digital image courtesy of the Getty Museum's Open Content Program.*

time lead the whole world to the truth of Spiritualism. We need not be in a hurry to prove it true; we need not spend our time and waste our money on it, for it will develop itself, and take care of itself. It is better to wait and let the thing take its natural course."

Complaints started to surface in 1863 when dissatisfied customers wrote to the *Banner* that Mumler lied when he guaranteed to send authentic spirit photographs to people at a distance. The Smith family of Stockton, California was very disappointed to receive six cards with a terribly blurred likeness of their deceased mother. They had followed directions exactly by enclosing $7.50, providing a photo of themselves and documenting the name, death date and age of the departed. The second try was equally expensive but no more satisfying than the first. Another situation occurred when Mr. Pollock of Boston was told that the spirit in his photograph was actually a manipulated copy of a portrait already taken by Mrs. Stuart. The original subject, Mrs. Peabody, was an elderly woman still living on Harrison Avenue. Mumler responded with the sweeping defense that spirits could not be held to earthly standards. He never guaranteed his results because he was simply an instrument used by higher powers.

The late 1860s were some of the most challenging years in Mumler's life. His Boston customers had became more discerning, especially when he was asking for a hefty ten dollars per photograph. In a strategic move, the Mumlers relocated to New York, where the business did well until he was brought to trial on charges of fraud. After hearing riveting testimony on both sides, with P.T. Barnum as a key witness for the prosecution, Judge Dowling dismissed the case, even though he was morally troubled by Mumler's profession.

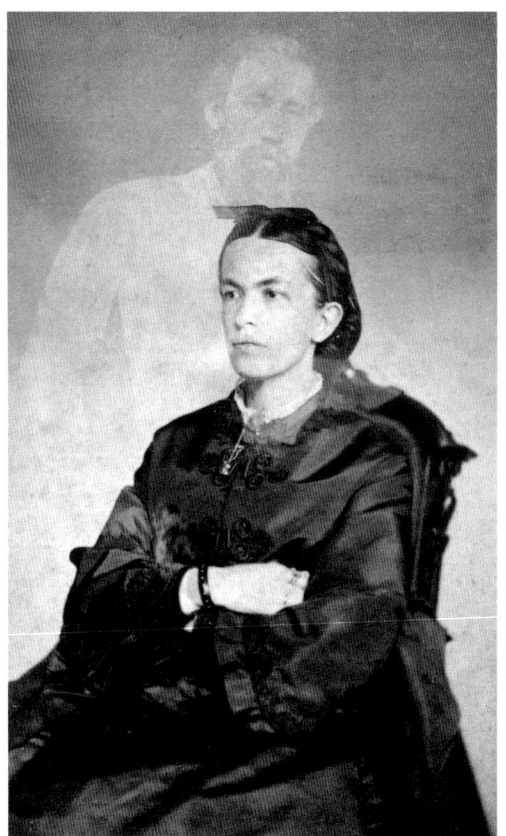

The shadowy figure of Charles Crowell stands behind the chair of his sister. Fanny often had visions of Charley. "Mrs. Conant" by William H. Mumler. *Courtesy of the J. Paul Getty Museum, Los Angeles.*

Back in Boston by 1870, the couple lived on West Springfield Street in a house belonging to Hannah's mother. It was a new decade with improved opportunities. Mrs. Mumler gave some of her attention to treating disease by the laying on of hands, but William still relied on her input in the studio because her magnetic powers seemed to encourage spirits to participate. Fanny Conant visited on several occasions and was thoroughly convinced that the process was a breakthrough into the spirit world. Besides the photograph featuring her spirit brother, she was thrilled with other sittings that produced images of transparent flowers. Perhaps the most personal was one that included Vashti, a petite Native American spirit that had suffered a terrible death at the 1871 massacre at the Yellow Stone River. Now a playful spirit guide, she was pictured standing close to the seated medium. Reproductions of the photograph became bestsellers at the *Banner* bookstore.

William's most famous client in January 1875 was a dowdy woman wearing a long veil that completely hid her features. "Mrs. Lindall"—really Mary Todd Lincoln—posed but later seemed to be disappointed in the resulting photograph. She turned for advice to Mrs. Mumler, who became entranced immediately. Under the influence of the spirit of a young man, Hannah said, "Mother, if you cannot recognize Father, then show the picture to Robert." That spirit message from her deceased son apparently convinced Mrs. Lincoln. The photograph in question showed Mrs. Lincoln seated in her widow's attire. The transparent image of a bearded man appeared to be standing behind her chair with his hands placed gently on her shoulders. There was no doubt that this was the martyred president, expressing his tender concern for his wife. Without hesitation, Mumler made sure that this compelling vignette was circulated and offered for sale.

By the end of the 1870s, William Mumler had moved on to producing engraved plates by means of photography. His company enjoyed commercial success unblemished by controversy.

The Transition of Mrs. Conant: 1875

Facts magazine paid a well-deserved tribute to Fanny shortly after her passing on August 5, 1875. It stated: "Mrs Conant is considered the best medium for spiritual communications on this continent." For over twenty years, she had been the public face of the Message Department through which she received ten thousand communications from the spirit world. She had always been physically delicate, so it came as no surprise when she was incapacitated during the spring of 1875. Her many friends sent wishes for a speedy recovery, but this was her final illness. Expressions of respect for her tireless work in the Public Circles poured in to the *Banner* office. Even the *Globe* printed a testimonial in which she was praised for her interest in all classes of people.

The private funeral rites at her Waltham Street home expanded to a formal sendoff at Parker Memorial Hall. Then Isaac Rich, a trusted friend and co-worker, presided at her graveside service. As the newly appointed proprietor of her lot, it was also his duty to set aside a space for her emotionally troubled husband, who had been committed to an insane asylum in Taunton. John Conant died a few months later and was interred beside his wife.

A small article in the *Banner* in early January 1876 announced that the spirit of Mrs. Conant was preparing an account of her reception in the next world. She said that Theodore Parker, the president of her special spirit band, had already extended every courtesy to her. Her Native American–style lodge fronted on a meadow that was the favorite exercise area of Carlo, her faithful companion. Mrs. Conant's fans asked the new medium in charge of the *Banner* circles to encourage the spirit of Fanny to manifest herself more frequently. Unfortunately, except for a recorded appearance to Luther Colby, Fanny did not reveal any more about her eternal home.

The Medium Who Refused to Accept Boundaries: Maud E. Lord (1852–1924)

When she emerged on the Boston scene in the 1870s, Mrs. Maud E. Lord carried herself like a lady with impeccable breeding. A tall, robust woman known for her exquisite manners, she possessed a complex personality. Clients little realized that her genteel bearing was her way of compensating for early traumas. Her lengthy memoir, *Psychic Light, Continuity of Law and Life*, published in 1904, detailed her dysfunctional childhood, as well as her incredible experiences. Her story owned a legitimacy that was lacking in many of the mediums who were starting to arrive on the Boston scene.

Born in West Virginia, Maud Barrock was the daughter of a Methodist mother from a slaveholding family and a Baptist father who had no tolerance for anything he could not prove. Attendance at church and school was curtailed when her parents discovered that she was carrying on lively conversations with invisible playmates. Her father thought this innocent activity showed the devil's influence. A sympathetic neighbor took her in after finding her beaten and half-clad body by the side of the road one wintry evening. Over the course of the next years, she taught herself to read and write, even though she was convinced that her spirit friends were her prime instructors. Maud, while still a teen, decided to move to Illinois, where she found her calling as a professional medium. From the beginning, she

The Rejection of Boundaries

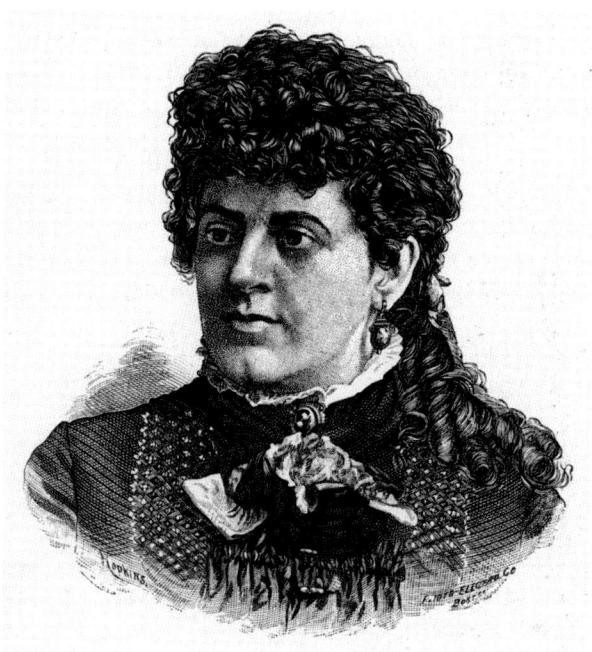

Maud Lord rose from poverty to success as a medium. Many spirit children visited her séances. *Boston Public Library.*

depended on three spirit guides by the names of Clarence and Jesse Wilbur, two deceased brothers, and Snowdrop, a young Native American spirit girl. Their influence filled the void created by her abusive family.

Having dodged a prearranged marriage in 1868, Maud then made her own poor choice by selecting Albert A. Lord, a superficial young man with a predisposition for jealous rages. She should have listened when his own mother indicated her misgivings. This older woman's view of her daughter-in-law was also quite perceptive, referring to the positive and then negative mood swings that kept the household in constant turmoil. The union was a sorry mix of misunderstandings and verbal battles, but the birth of a daughter, Maud Alberta, brought deep comfort. Mrs. Lord gradually realized that the spirit of Clarence was urging her to hone her abilities in other cities, such as Chicago and New York. He gave her the recipe for a health tonic, Golden Discovery: A Clairvoyant Liver Remedy and Blood Purifier, which made her a tidy profit when sold in many urban pharmacies. The biggest boost to her self-confidence occurred when she filed for divorce and won. Freed from the clutches of an unstable husband, she arrived in Boston in 1874. Her spirit guides assured her that she would find happiness.

While renting some modest rooms on Tremont Street, Mrs. Lord was hired by Manager Lucien Bigelow to hold a séance in the fashionable

Continental Hotel. He surmised that celebrities such as the poet John G. Whittier, Governor Rice and other dignitaries would relish this offbeat entertainment. To test the medium, Mrs. Bigelow requested that her own lace cap be transported across the darkened parlor. Maud pronounced the deed almost accomplished while two men held her hands down. As the lamps were lit, the bonnet was seen neatly tied around the face of a grandfather clock. Mrs. Bigelow swore that she had felt invisible hands undoing the strings. This interlude led to social connections with many of the best people in Boston and surrounding towns.

After an extensive road trip, Mrs. Lord found lodgings on Milford Street, a more stylish location. Before long, she was practicing her unique brand of séance. First, she placed herself inside the circle of participants and frequently clapped her hands. This was to prove that, by keeping her fingers occupied, she could not be accused of producing any manifestations. She then called out to any spirit who might be present. As if on cue, soft whispers would start to emerge from all corners of the darkened room. The voices would then become individualized. They might include the spirits of adults presenting details about their childhoods or the lilting tones of invisible adolescents who might burst into song at any moment. More ghostly voices would join the others until a gentle, persistent hum surrounded the circle. Many people at the séance were moved to tears when they thought that they heard the spirits of departed relatives carrying on conversations.

At other times, Mrs. Lord arranged to have large phosphorescent globes move slowly through the air, revealing a spirit face that might look like a deceased friend. The audience members discovered that some of their jewelry was being gently removed and placed on the fingers or necks of someone else. Guitars were strummed by invisible fingers as a chorus of bodiless singers warbled a hymn. Sitting close together in the dark chamber, the usually formal men and women became conditioned to having invisible hands pat their shoulders, stroke their hair or rub their backs. Mrs. Rudd, a medium working for the *Banner of Light*, attended many sessions and gave her stamp of approval.

While all was going well professionally, Maud's private life was in chaos. In May 1878, the *Boston Globe* ran a sensational bit of news. The popular Mrs. Lord had suddenly disappeared while on her way to the Old Colony railroad to catch a train to Brockton. She was said to have carried on her person several hundred dollars worth of jewelry plus a substantial amount of cash. Her friends volunteered the information that her ex-husband had recently come to the city in an effort to rekindle their romance. The mystery deepened, despite the valiant efforts of local mediums and police detectives to find her. Fortunately, her ten-year-old daughter was safe in the custody of a friend from the South End.

Maud reappeared after an absence of over five weeks. She offered a melodramatic explanation that included a lengthy voyage to England, where strange things happened. Somehow she was able to escape from the evildoers and miraculously, without much money in her possession, return to Boston. Here she was forced into a hasty marriage with one Thomas Mitchell, a wealthy man who had been infatuated with her for months. Now with the title of Mrs. Lord-Mitchell, she continued on with her séances. Maud was busier than ever because people were interested in seeing the lady who had experienced so much trauma. After a few months, she filed for a divorce from her second husband and was granted her freedom. She never did explain what had really transpired during those weeks when she was missing.

Her final address in Boston was a fine home on Chester Park in the South End. Her guide, Clarence, had correctly informed her that she would be able to buy it at a below-market rate. After trusting a dishonest friend with some of her savings, Maud was almost cheated out of purchasing the dwelling that the immortals had promised to her, but eventually, she and her daughter started keeping house. Financial support poured in from ordinary spiritualists, as well as professional lecturers. Her apparent sincerity and need for protection brought out the best in the community.

Maud's séances here gave even more satisfaction. Mrs. E.J. Pike from Roxbury was thrilled to report that in the dark, she sensed the presence of many spirit children who climbed on her lap, patted the cheeks of other members of the audience and happily prattled about their happy life. A spirit uncle who had been a sea captain cordially kissed her hand. At the intermission, when the lights had come on and the audience was enjoying refreshments, the twenty attendees compared their reactions. One woman stated that she thought she detected the presence of a friend who had committed suicide. Rather than being frightened, the lady assured everyone that she was delighted to be reunited with a loved one who might have been condemned to everlasting fire.

Adjusting to his new role, Clarence became the spirit manager of the home. His duties included loosening the lids stuck on jars of food and removing corks from bottles. Miss Emma J. Huff, a friend and boarder, often heard the two spirit brothers conversing with the other immortal, the playful Snowdrop. This petite invisible being became especially helpful when one servant, Bridget O'Leary, kept stocking her basket with food from the Lords' pantry. Appearing in the kitchen doorway so that she could be seen, Snowdrop caused a bag filled with clothespins to empty themselves on top of the cowering maid. Bridget's screams drew in Mrs. Lord, who, remembering her own past, straightened out the situation but did not fire the girl. Maud Alberta, now a very lively preteen, easily forged friendships with the spirit children who appeared to her. Like her mother before her, she completely believed in her powers to see invisible beings. Sometimes neighbors who walked by the house saw Mrs. Lord playing her heavy Steinway piano. It seemed, they said, to lift off the floor, spin and turn in time to the music.

By the 1880s, Mrs. Lord was ready to move out West. Very sorry to see her leave, 1,500 guests assembled in Tremont Hall, where they tendered her a magnificent reception. The speakers paying tribute were a diverse collection of Catholics, Congregationalists, atheists and believers. Local spiritualists eagerly followed her subsequent adventures. Her third marriage was a success. J.S. Drake, a contractor and builder, possessed an even temperament and shared her values. Wherever she traveled, she always looked on Boston with great affection.

Chapter 4
A TALE OF TWO TOWNS

Winchester and Stoneham

There are two towns, Winchester and Stoneham, just north of Boston that share a border in addition to being adjacent to the Middlesex Fells, a picturesque tract of wilderness that has been set aside to remain forever open. Both take up approximately the same land space of about six square miles.

Winchester, formally incorporated as a town in 1850, is a combination of the southern part of Woburn, a piece of Medford and a smaller section of West Cambridge, today's Arlington. Because of its lovely setting and important railway connections to Boston, it attracted people who worked in the city but also wanted the beauties of the country. The first residents of the new town developed a community that was very conscious of its civic responsibilities. Charles Francis Adams, chairman of the Metropolitan Park Commission in the late nineteenth century, commented that the town possessed a healthy awareness of how to manage itself.

Stoneham separated from Charlestown in 1725 and officially became independent. On the east and west, two ranges of hills protected the rolling countryside that lay between them. Spot Pond in the southern part of town was considered by local historian William B. Stevens to be the "most beautiful water scene in the vicinity of Boston." Residents were dissatisfied with the railroad connections to the urban center until improvements were made after 1890. It was a manufacturing town of many shoe factories that still maintained a sense of living in a semi-rural environment. Because many people were focused on producing a similar product, there was a strong feeling of community.

During the 1870s, spiritualism had an impact on both locations. Winchester dealt with two very different men who called themselves spiritualists: J. Frank Baxter, a flamboyant teacher, and Edward A. Brackett, a brilliant—if not eccentric—artist.

Stoneham had a more serene experience. Edward Whittier, a newspaper editor, encouraged the movement. C. Fannie Allyn, an inspirational lecturer, had very progressive ideas but knew how to fit into a working-class setting.

The Medium Who Led Two Lives: J. Frank Baxter (1841–1904)

J. Frank Baxter got into a great deal of trouble in the town where he had hoped to spend most of his life. Everything had started out so brilliantly when he began teaching in Winchester, but then he fell out of favor. Perhaps if the School Committee had investigated his early days in Plymouth, the entire mess could have been avoided.

Born in the city of the Pilgrims, Josiah Baxter believed that he had felt the touch of spirits since 1848, when he was seven years old. He was also blessed with a golden singing voice and a comprehensive memory. During childhood, he had ignored the invisible world because he knew that his yeoman relatives would disapprove. Frank set his sights on becoming a teacher because the Bridgewater Normal School offered a free education to graduates who pledged to serve in the public schools for several years. In 1859, armed with a diploma, Baxter was hired in his hometown. Curiosity got the better of him when several of his friends dared him to participate in some tests of spiritualism that they wanted to try on their own. He agreed yet secretly wondered if his early memories would be awakened.

In 1860, these twenty-five amateurs rented a small hall, decorated it and formed circles. They promised to meet twice a week until they either contacted spirits or concluded that this type of communication was impossible. The young men and women chose seats at several round tables, joined hands and sat silently in complete darkness for hours. More than four months passed without the slightest hint of reaching the boundaries of eternity. Then, tiny showers of raps were heard in various parts of the hall. Baxter felt compelled to take up pencil and paper and was inspired to draw a seating plan with each person's name attached to a chair. This arrangement, dictated by unidentified beings, made all the difference. When the young people sang, the tables tipped back and forth while making thumps that sounded like a bass drum. Other beats, bangs and taps joined in on every chorus, leading everyone to feel that the spirits were playing with the harmony.

One evening, Frank sensed that he was being lifted by invisible forces. He begged his companions not to let go of him, but the pull upward was irresistible. After touching the ceiling, he was allowed to descend back down the twelve feet to his place at the table. The same type of levitation occurred eighteen times over the course of nine meetings. He collected some of the cut paper garlands festooning the overhead arches and was aware of forms in gauzy robes floating around above him. It had not occurred to him that the spirits were training him to become a medium.

On June 25, 1861, Baxter returned late to his rented room, where he was suddenly seized with a persistent tingling in his right arm. After grabbing his writing equipment, he waited patiently in the unlit chamber. Twenty minutes later, he transcribed a rambling discourse from a being that said that he was the spirit of Deacon Judson R. Phelps from Southwick. Testily complaining of having been crushed to death while tearing down a barn on his property, he wanted Baxter's sympathy. The stunned young man contacted the deceased farmer's postmaster in order to validate the story. He received a confirmation yet kept the experience to himself. Other experiences encouraged him to hold séances for friends in the Plymouth area.

Once Eliza Holmes, one of his followers, became Mrs. Baxter in 1865, the couple moved to Nantucket and then points north as teaching positions opened up. Frank devoted many evenings and much of his summer break to appearances at urban lecture halls, where he was lauded for his clairvoyant abilities. When they entered the 1870s, Eliza and Frank sensed that Winchester was going to be their next move because the town was in the market for an educator with talent and a love for the classics. After his interview, Baxter knew that he had made a favorable impression. The School Committee of 1872 wrote, "We were fortunately able to fill a vacancy by securing the services of Mr. J. Frank Baxter, whose reputation as a teacher was already established." And indeed, the board members were justified in thinking that he was a scholar who would be devoted to his students. Each June for several years, Frank was reappointed along with the other qualified staff members. His excellent evaluations were enhanced by tributes from his students who considered him to be a friend as well as an instructor.

During the summer of 1875, Baxter was basking in the good press he was receiving when he performed as a celebrated trance medium. His lectures throughout Massachusetts, into the mid-Atlantic states and even in West

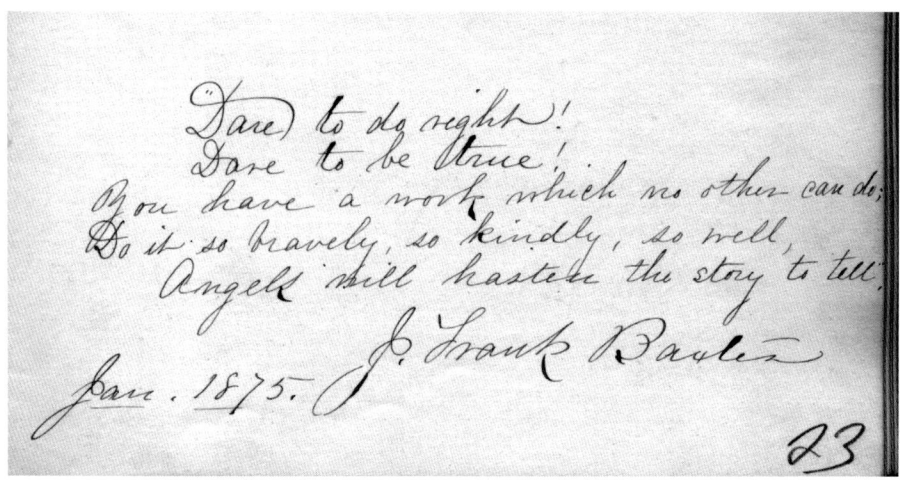

Virginia drew packed houses. A testimonial published by Boston's often-critical *Spiritual Scientist* newspaper lauded him for including many details concerning his spirit contacts. No detail was overlooked as Frank stated manner, time and place of death, as well as little-known events. The paper suggested that spiritualism would blossom anywhere that Baxter worked or visited—and this was exactly the problem. As his speaking engagements became more numerous, his fame spread. Stories started to travel back to the town that had given him his day job.

A somewhat testy Winchester School Committee sent its maverick teacher a written expression of its concerns in October 1876. His extracurricular activities were deemed inappropriate, and he was asked to cease and desist. But Frank did not respond. By the turn of the following year, the officials learned that he was still pursuing his own agenda. The news that he was lecturing in adjacent communities led the committee to fire off another dispatch. This time it was stated that the students were complaining that he was often exhausted. Because his "hobby" was draining the energy out of his teaching, the board ordered him to forgo lectures and séances during the school year. Baxter denied fatigue but promised that he would acquiesce. The board thought that this was the end of the discussion.

The issue of spiritualism boiled over again by the end of the summer. In August 1877, Frank was billed as one of the headliners at a camp meeting at Lake Pleasant near the town of Montague. There was also mention that he was from Winchester. Speaking before a huge crowd of day-trippers, he electrified his audience with message after message from the departed. Then came the most astounding revelation. He conveyed a folksy communication

A Tale of Two Towns

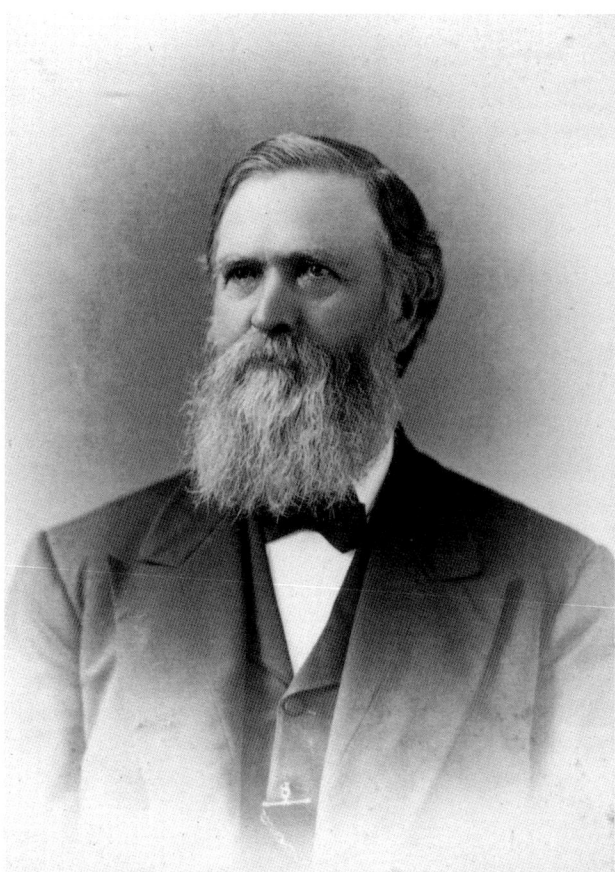

Opposite: Mr. Baxter was a great favorite with the town scholars. This autograph album displays his fine penmanship. *Winchester Archives*.

Left: Mr. George S. Littlefield of the school committee tried to reason with Baxter, but the spiritualist would not take heed. *Winchester Archives*.

from a departed African American, Abe Bunter of Williamstown, who had achieved some modest fame. The day laborer had possessed such a thick skull that he could split a plank with a blow from his forehead. Born a slave in New York State, Bunter had earned extra money by putting on this show of strength. The crowd clapped and cheered until a man in the audience stood to announce that Bunter was still among the living. Two years previously, someone had written a premature obituary that had been published but never retracted. Baxter fell back, trying to stem the damage by accusing some inferior spirits of delivering false information. Local papers such as the *Greenfield Gazette* picked up the exposé, which then made its way to the Boston press.

The notoriety was intense. Frank was quoted in the *Springfield Daily Union* as saying that a group of African American immortals had enticed him to perform an old-time spiritual. Under their influence, he had received the

Bunter message. They clearly were being mischievous and out to do him harm. The *Turner Falls Reporter* did not mince words when it denounced him as a fraud. Yet the *Sunday Herald* of August 26 rose to his defense by reminding its readers of his reputation as one of the most respected mediums in New England. Back in Winchester, the committee swiftly reacted by ordering him to explain himself by August 30 in the faint hope that the press had overstated everything. It was just days away from the opening of the fall term.

The teacher passionately defended his right to be a spiritualist and to exercise his psychic powers. But his additional admission of experiencing levitation or, as the committee report stated, "sailing through the air," seriously impacted his case. There was no other possibility than to dismiss him. He was not terminated for his beliefs but because he had openly committed fraud. As the fallout continued to spread, Frank sent an open letter protesting his innocence to the *Woburn Journal*, which he signed, "Yours for Justice and Honor." On September 15, the same paper printed a response in which a Baxter supporter asked rhetorically about the right of a teacher to have his own convictions.

The *Banner* defended him without reservation. The editor then remarked that fifty of Baxter's former pupils had brought him fruit, flowers and two framed pictures as tokens of their respect. Young Mr. Blaisdell, the spokesman for the scholars, had expressed their confidence in him as a man and their gratitude to him as a teacher. The whole story continued to percolate. In 1879, the radical *Boston Investigator* could not resist mentioning that "Orthodox bigots" had thrust Baxter out of their school. After this episode, Frank never taught again.

Baxter prospered on the lecture circuit. He was always regarded as a stimulating speaker. Sustained by a formidable drive to succeed plus many hearty endorsements from the *Banner*, he traveled all over America and Canada season after season. When he was engaged to speak at Boston's Berkeley Hall, the *Globe* of February 23, 1891, stated that the main floor and balconies were so crowded that scores of eager listeners had to remain standing. People in the audience responded with cries of "That's my uncle" and so forth when he called out the names of spirits who were present.

Almost fifteen years after leaving his teaching position, Baxter and his family were living in Charlestown near the Bunker Hill Monument. Eliza was deeply involved in volunteering at the Boston Spiritualist Ladies' Aid Society. Frank was doing special appearances at campground meetings and conventions in addition to keeping up with his exhausting schedule. The town of Winchester had moved on to more important topics, but every once in a while, someone would mention the spiritualist who had caused such a stir.

The Spiritualist Who Had to Prove Everything: Edward A. Brackett (1818–1908)

Edward A. Brackett fell in love with spiritualism during the last decades of his long life. He had scrutinized it as fully as he had examined his other diverse interests and was gratified that it came close to fulfilling his search for truth. His obituary in the *Winchester Star* summed him up as "a most remarkable man of brilliant and diversified attainments." The praise was accurate, but there was, of course, much more to his story.

This son of Quaker parents knew from the beginning that he was supposed to do something important with his life. When he worked as a tradesman's apprentice during his teen years in Cincinnati, he realized that he was just trying to please his father. He was miserable because he was suppressing his need to create art. By the 1830s, Edward was molding clay into naturalistic shapes. Then he felt confident enough to carve portrait busts in marble. The next step was to establish himself in New York, but he failed to find enough clients. During the hot summer of 1841, he landed in Boston because he believed his luck was changing.

Few commissions were forthcoming. Despite this, he married a girl named Amanda Folger, rented a studio on Park Street and churned out inexpensive crayon likenesses in order to make a living. His practical wife suggested that moving to the suburbs would ease their financial troubles. South Woburn was selected because it was a few miles north of Boston and had the reputation of being a good place to raise a family. They bought a few acres in 1848 for next to nothing and then added more that were rich in hardwood trees and evergreens. In 1850, their remote parcel became part of the new town of Winchester.

Sometime between 1850 and 1854, Brackett decided to build a very unusual home on their Highland Avenue land. He felt that a house had to be compatible with the lifestyle and personality of the inhabitants. For inspiration, he turned to a recently published plan book that was a how-to manual on the construction of octagon houses. Oren S. Fowler's *A Home for All: Or a Cheap, Convenient and Superior Mode of Building* (1849) appealed to both his imagination and his pocket book. The eight-sided shape avoided the use of sharp angles, thus creating spacious rooms that allowed in a maximum amount of sunlight and a more liberal circulation of air. By using a system of interlocking horizontal boards to create a solid wall, there was no need for an expensive under-skeleton. The rough planks were inexpensive and probably came from one of the mills along the Aberjona River. Brackett designed his home to be a creative mix of complete and partial octagons with the

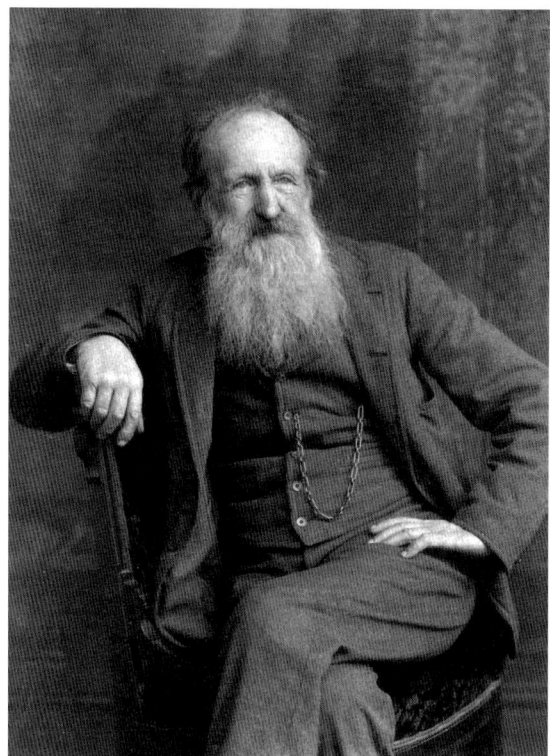

Left: Edward A. Brackett became an enthusiastic believer in spirit communication. Conversing with his spirit niece, Bertha, brought him great happiness. *Winchester Archives.*

Below: Brackett built his octagon house so that it would be bathed in sunlight and filled with fresh breezes. *Winchester Archives.*

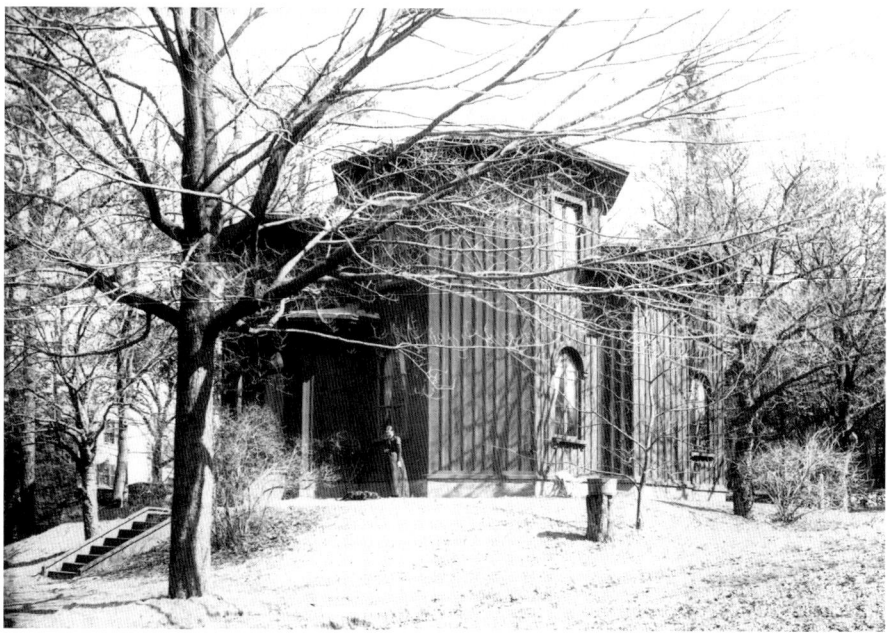

different levels of the roof adding interest. It was dubbed the "Crow's Nest" because of its shape.

Edward now had to focus on the art that had always meant so much to him. With financial backing from his artist brother, Walter, he produced his masterpiece in marble, *Shipwrecked Mother and Child* (circa 1852). This emotional sculpture depicted a drowned nude woman clasping her baby. Bostonians flocked to see it when it was put on display, which was a boost to his career. In 1859, his sympathetic bust of John Brown, the abolitionist who led the unsuccessful raid on Harper's Ferry, underscored his antislavery leanings. He mentored Edmonia Lewis, the first African American sculptor of note, and found the energy to serve in the First Massachusetts Cavalry during the beginning of the Civil War.

In 1871, Amanda died, leaving Brackett to write some tender poetry about their relationship and her loving concern. On a professional level, he was in the process of giving up his art career in order to concentrate on his role in the Massachusetts Fish and Game Commission. The State Fish Hatchery was housed in a chapel-style building not far from the octagon house. His personal life was enriched in 1872, when he married Elizabeth Folger Bellville, the daughter of Amanda's sister. Together, they would explore spiritualism.

The Power of the Invisible

Edward Brackett had already turned two popular "sciences" inside out. Phrenology, the belief that a person's character could be discovered by studying the configurations of the human skull, had caught his attention about 1844, when he was sculpting the bust of Washington Allston, a Cambridge artist. Brackett was fascinated that physical bumps, indentations or a broad or narrow brow might be a good indication of personality. When he built his house, he used the patterns developed by Oren Fowler, a noted phrenologist. He was in harmony with Fowler's outlook, as well as his designs.

Mesmerism was the second system that intrigued Edward. As a young man in 1839, he and his friends had taken turns hypnotizing one another. In Boston, he continued his experiments in hopes of discovering that there was an electric current connecting the mesmerizer with his subject. He finally decided that the altered state was produced by means of telepathy. Up for the challenge, he tried out his theory on family members, most likely on his first wife, Amanda. She began to deliver random messages that were of little importance. He dropped his inquiries to get busy doing other things. When he observed a medium becoming entranced decades later, he wondered if that condition was another version of hypnosis.

One of the first real séances that Edward attended was conducted by Mrs. Herman Fay, a medium with a specialty. She featured physical materializations, which meant that spirits in human form came out of the cabinet where she sat and mingled with the audience. When Brackett settled himself in a chair in her parlor on West Newton Street, he was not sure what to expect. The lighting in the room was dim, which made it impossible to see details. A white-draped female figure came toward him and spoke so hoarsely that he barely heard that she was mouthing: "I am Maggie Brackett." This meant little to him, so he shook her hand politely before she retreated back to the cabinet. Mrs. Fay announced, "The spirit of your first wife is here!" A petite form entered the room, but Edward pronounced her figure to be too small and thin. She retired and was replaced in a few minutes by a being that was at least a foot taller. Quickly embracing him, the spirit woman talked in generalities about their life in Winchester. Although he had the fleeting thought that the being resembled Mrs. Fay, Brackett was moved to have so many memories come to the surface. He went back home pondering the possibility that he might have connected with the beyond.

The experience that broke down all reserve took place during another séance at Mrs. Fay's. Brackett was captivated by an attractive young being dressed in a luminous, close-fitting garment that left her arms bare. Her long hair drifted past her slight shoulders. Speaking in clear tones, she called herself Bertha as she placed her hand gently on his arm. From the cabinet, Mrs. Fay called out that he should think about the members of his family, initially a very puzzling statement. Brackett suddenly flung his arms around the form standing in front of him. Appearing to be in her twenties, this spirit had to be Bertha Belle, a younger brother's daughter, who passed away in 1865 when she was only four. She had matured in eternity and now was transformed into a perfect representation of girlhood from the top of her delicate face to the tips of her small feet. Over the course of other meetings, the spirit of Bertha delighted him not only with her charming appearance and sunny disposition but also her coquettish demeanor.

Elizabeth, his second wife, often accompanied her husband to séances, especially at the home of Helen Berry, who lived not far from Mrs. Fay. They brought along their daughter, also named Bertha, who felt entirely comfortable dealing with materializations. Sarah Jane Newton, wife of their friend Alonzo, sat with the Brackett family as the spirit of Bertha walked out of Miss Berry's cabinet. The being raised her arms above her head while rubbing her hands lightly together until a flower dripping with dew appeared. Then she gathered her namesake in a fond embrace before leading the ten-year-old into the cabinet. The parents were startled but reassured to hear their own Bertha laughing. Mrs. Newton wrote Edward a testimonial letter in which she commented that his spirit niece looked intensely human but was more beautiful than if made of ordinary flesh and blood. Elizabeth, a few months later, penned a description of her spirit relative emerging slowly from a faint white light that increased in size.

In 1887, Brackett was comfortable enough with his belief in spiritualism to invite Mrs. Ross, a Boston medium, to the "Crow's Nest." Several local lawyers and other friends attended while Elizabeth played the hostess. Among them was Alonzo Newton, who described the event, which was then published in the *Banner* in May. Brackett had created an impromptu cabinet by hanging curtains across one area of the parlor. Over the course of the evening, twelve materialized forms appeared one by one and delivered interesting but not particularly personal messages. The Bracketts' daughter thought that she recognized her spirit cousin in the subdued light. Mr. Newton was completely sure of the honesty of Mrs. Ross, even though this was a more scaled-down version of her usual performance. It seemed that the Winchester neighbors were entertained but not willing to commit to further investigation.

Mr. Brackett gained great satisfaction in participating in formal séances. Whether promenading up and down with his spirit Bertha—much to the enjoyment of his colleague, John Wetherbee, and other believers—or sharing these experiences with his empathetic wife and daughter, he was convinced that every ghostly appearance was authentic. One of his favorite moments took place at Helen Berry's house when a cloud-like substance expanded until it was about four to five feet tall. Out from it stepped his spirit niece in all her youthful beauty.

All of his determinations were based on a confidence in his own powers of observation. He assumed that the years spent honing his visual skills would make deception almost impossible. In addition, he thought that his minute examination of phrenology and mesmerism would help him to detect any counterfeit physical materialization. And there was his openness to a wonderful possibility that all these sights were legitimate. Brackett's fascinating endorsement of spiritualism, *Materialized Apparitions* (1885), was one of several books and articles published in support of the movement. He wanted to share the experiences that brought him to a level of fulfillment that he had never enjoyed before. Many Winchester residents appreciated Brackett's huge talent, his work as fish commissioner and his wholehearted dedication to the town. His interest in the spirit world was seen as an eccentricity that did not cause harm.

A Real Confession

In 1892, a dedicated supporter of spiritualism found it important to compile some exposés in S*ome Account of the Vampires of Onset*. One section borrowed part of an 1880s article from the *Boston Herald*. Being interviewed under a cloak of anonymity, a former actress revealed her participation in some of the séances frequented by Edward Brackett. She was one of several theater people who were employed from time to time by a few Boston mediums. Her particular assignment was to impersonate the spirit niece of the artist. Spirit Bertha's costumes, hairstyle and winning ways were carefully orchestrated. When she worked for Mrs. Amanda Cowen of Tremont Street, the performer perfected the illusion of appearing spontaneously in the séance room. This was facilitated by stretching black curtains on rods and hanging them a few inches from the walls. The audience never noticed that the room was smaller than it should have been. While the medium distracted the people, the actress would feel her way behind the heavy drapes. She would carefully count off the number of seats until she reached Brackett's. Then, with a sprightly flourish, she would spring out to grab his hand. His joy was evident as they would embrace and engage in conversation. Asking him to concentrate on something in some other part of the parlor, for example, she would then disappear the way that she had come. Sadly, he did not realize that Mrs. Cowen had duped him.

The Stoneham Setting

One of the most popular stories supposedly circulating in Stoneham in August 1870 was reproduced in the *Banner of Light* under the heading, "A Remarkable Case of Spirit Sight." The narrative bordered on the saccharine. It seems that an eight-year-old child went into a store on Main

Street and saw the spirit form of a baby resting near the feet of a woman who was waiting for her order. When the youngster mentioned the little one, the customer was upset because she had recently, as the piece reported, "lost an infant by death." The child played with the spirit until it slowly vanished from sight. Though not a spiritualist, the mother was comforted that she had been in the presence of her departed son. "How cheering would be the assurance," the story ended, "if the departed are in reality around us on earth and loving us." While the incident was probably fictional, it did demonstrate the attitude of many Stoneham residents toward spiritualism.

THE HIDDEN SPIRITUALIST: MOSES A. DOW (1810–1886)

Moses A. Dow was a very wealthy Boston entrepreneur, prominent spiritualist and editor of the *Waverley Magazine,* one of the most popular periodicals of the Victorian era. He also invested heavily in real estate, the Dow Building being one of his best projects. Built during the Civil War in 1864, this brick edifice with a mansard roof became the most striking landmark in Central Square. The public library was one of the first notable tenants. The report from 1867 was lyrical in conveying the good tidings: "From a cramped and inconvenient room, [the library] has passed into the best location which the

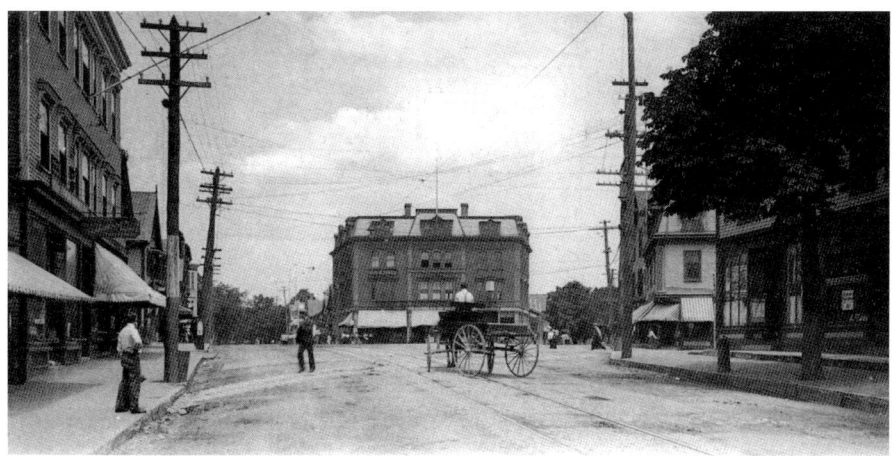

The Dow Building in Central Square is a Stoneham landmark. It was the investment project of a spiritualist. *Author's collection.*

town can afford for such a purpose, furnishing unsurpassed conveniences to those applying for its benefits." In 1874, the *Stoneham Sentinel* news office was doing business there with the intention of supplying "good printing of every description." By 1882, the spacious hall on the second floor had been fitted up as the Stoneham headquarters for the Grand Army of the Republic (GAR). The Independent Order of Red Men, a fraternal organization, held its meetings in the public space in the 1880s, as did several other groups. Mr. Dow may have visited his building, but no record has survived. In 1864, he was busy with his publishing business, as well as several other construction projects. There is a likelihood that, as an investigator and subsequent believer in spiritualism, he was very aware that the town was favorable to the movement.

THE SPIRIT-PORTRAIT OF MABEL WARREN

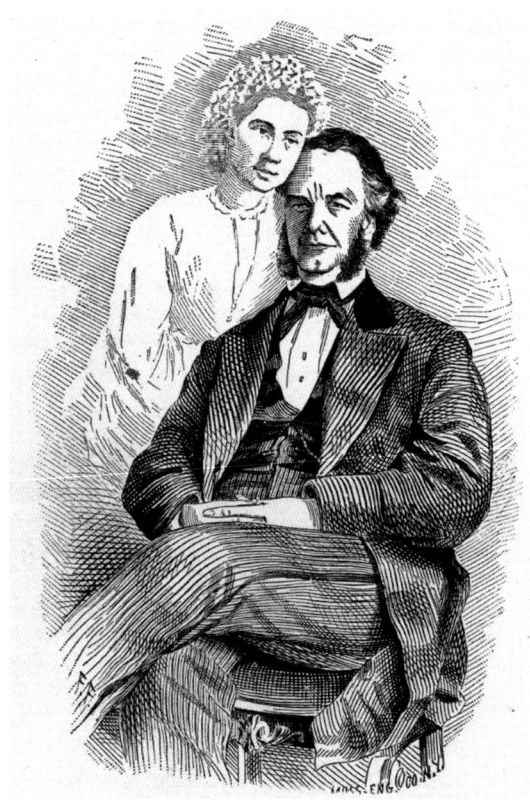

This drawing of a spirit photograph depicts Moses Dow and his talented spirit-employee, Mabel Warren. *Boston Public Library.*

In an 1875 article in the *Banner,* Moses reminisced about his introduction to the era of spiritualism. He admitted that when he heard about the Fox sisters and their rappings, he had hoped that more would come of these performances than entertainment for the public. He recognized that spiritualism could free the human mind from many false beliefs. Rather than plunge in, he had watched others take an active part in exploring the new mysteries since he feared being distracted from the responsibilities of his work. Yet he kept track of the early activists such as LaRoy Sunderland and Alonzo E. Newton, who were publishing spirit-friendly newspapers. He remained on the outskirts of commitment.

By 1862, he had met Mabel Warren, a poised young woman and recent high school graduate. Because of all her sterling qualities and evident talent, she was hired as his assistant. Dow came to regard her as an adopted daughter, her own father and mother having died while she was a child. Mabel's sudden passing in 1870 became the subject of a séance held at his Charlestown home by Mrs. Higgins, a medium, and his own housekeeper, a spiritualist. In a heartfelt remembrance of the event recorded in the February 13, 1875 *Banner*, Dow stated that one of the invisible beings guiding Mrs. Higgins testified that the spirit of Mabel was present: "She is sitting on the banks of a beautiful river, and she is surrounded with beautiful flowers and has a flower in her hand that is for you. She loves you because you were so good to her."

More interchanges at séances in Boston and Saratoga, New York, took place, making Dow eager to contact Mrs. Mumler, the spirit photographer's wife. She, of course, advised him to pose for his portrait because Mabel had informed her that she would be in the studio adorned with a wreath of lilies and wearing a dress with a subtle pattern of stripes. After several failed attempts, Mumler was able to produce the photograph that he called his masterpiece. From that time on, Moses Dow became one of the most vocal supporters of spiritualism in the Boston area.

THE GRACIOUS BELIEVER: EDWARD TUCK WHITTIER (1819-1878)

It was about 1838 when young Edward Whittier first set eyes on the town of Stoneham. He had just been hired by the public schools after gaining some teaching experience in his native state of New Hampshire. His marriage to a local girl, Elizabeth Jane Young, strengthened the impression that he had found his real home. After a year as an instructor, he tried his hand at shoe making but did not have the patience to sit at a bench stitching leather for over ten hours a day. Then he opened a periodical and variety shop, where he sold two Boston papers, the *Daily Bee* and the *Herald*. Whittier's interest in the written word prodded him to invest in some second-hand presses and type. Already serving as the town postmaster since 1856, he opened a printing office in the back room of the Dike Building in the Square.

The Civil War tested Whittier's patriotism in the 1860s. More than four hundred men volunteered out of a population of fewer than three thousand souls. Edward and other Stoneham fathers actively promoted the cause that changed their untested sons into soldiers. He and Elizabeth were inconsolable when their eldest boys made the ultimate sacrifice. Charles died from wounds suffered at Antietam during 1862, and Leonard was struck down at Spottsylvania Court House in 1864. It is likely that Whittier became interested in spiritualism at this time in an effort to transcend his grief. It is certain that his allegiance was complete by the next decade.

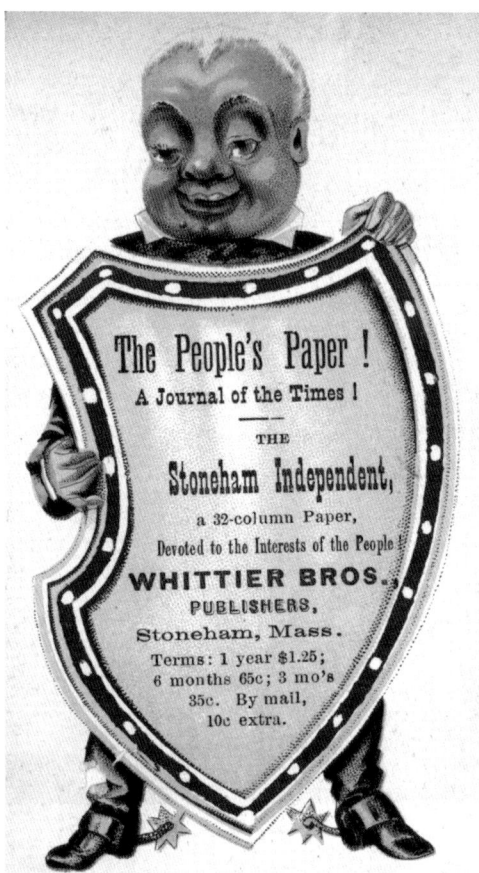

The *Stoneham Independent* was owned by the Whittier family. Edward, the father, was an ardent spiritualist. *Author's collection.*

A Spiritualist Newspaper in the Suburbs

The first issue of the *Stoneham Amateur* was distributed free of charge on March 21, 1870, to townspeople interested in local items, a bit of light fiction and some tidbits about the surrounding communities. It was written, set in type and printed by Edward Whittier and his two remaining sons, Frank and William, in their new building near the Dow Block. Within six weeks, Whittier was charging a small subscription fee because he knew that residents would not hesitate to pay for something they found valuable.

Whittier inserted an overt reference to his belief in the spirit world by using a unique header above the obituaries. People with Stoneham connections did not "die." Instead, they "Passed to Spirit Life." The uninitiated were not offended in reading this, and spiritualists appreciated the direct tie-in to an active immortality. Whether the departed was advanced in years or two months and thirteen days old like Mabel McFarland, the same words were used. These positive sentiments were also carved on a number of monuments erected in the Victorian part of Lindenwood Cemetery, the beautiful burying ground located in the western section of the town. Ira Gerry, an important businessman, "passed from earth to a higher life in his 70th year." The Joseph Leeds family all "passed" into eternity, as did an impressive array of shoe manufacturers and artisans.

As the mission of the *Amateur* matured, Edward maintained a neutral position toward other denominations. The People's Column, however, was an outlet for the strong opinions of other residents, particularly on this topic. One correspondent was incensed that another local paper printed the extract of an ultra-conservative sermon that degraded the movement. His rejoinder in August 1874 captured the attitude of much of the progressive community: "We are aware that some who have been spiritualists, or claimed to be such, have not done altogether right. But what of it? Does that alter the fact that spirits communicate with us at the present time? I look upon the matter as an established scientific fact, as much so as astronomy and geology."

In contrast, a writer calling himself a "Seed by the Wayside" pointed out the obligation to understand the true meaning of spiritualism and not be dazzled by flashy manifestations. His December 1874 letter offered a more restrained view: "The Spiritualism that purifies the heart and life is from above; but that which has a tendency to draw us away from God—to cast the Bible aside as worthless—to shut ourselves up in darkness—to tip tables, listen to raps on the wall or floor—Are all these things elevating, as partaking in any degree of Heaven's spirituality?"

Whittier practiced his own form of ecumenism by playing the organ at the Unitarian Church as well as running some of its fairs. Two years before he passed away, Whittier changed the name of the paper to the *Stoneham Independent*, which still exists today. His sons continued his work but were not inclined to embrace his religious views. William B. Stevens, the author of *A History of Stoneham*, stated the obvious when he said: "Mr. Whittier occupied a prominent position in the community by his strong avowal of spiritualism."

The Importance of a Welcoming Place

Harmony Hall on Main Street lived up to the meaning of its name every time spiritualist lecturers held their weekend meetings there. On July 8, 1871, the *Amateur* was gratified that "an interested and appreciative audience" had assembled to see the performance of Miss Jennie Leys, a young trance speaker who compared modern spiritualism to the revelations found in antiquity. In the spring of 1878, J. Frank Baxter spoke in Stoneham months before his situation in Winchester reached its unpleasant climax. His April 14 program was very well received as he lifted his voice in song before recounting some spirit messages intended for the audience. He spoke so eloquently about his beliefs that he was frequently invited back. These engagements fit well into his later career as an independent lecturer.

The practice of spiritualism became a part of everyday life and social gatherings. Private homes such as William Pierce's on the corner of Summer and Franklin Streets became temporary offices. Miss Sarah Appleton, a healing medium, had taken a room there and was available every Monday, Tuesday and Wednesday for an indefinite number of weeks. She was allowed exclusive use of the side parlor for the purpose of attending to patients. In 1874, Mrs. Manchester, "the celebrated and highly popular clairvoyant and eclectic physician," stayed at L.A. Fuller's on Franklin Street, next door to Drew & Buswell's shoe factory. She was available for appointments during which she cured those suffering from nervous disorders. And there was the occasion when a group of thirty Stoneham spiritualists were invited to a birthday party at the home of H.B. Cushman, the musical medium, in Melrose. In a great show of unity, people joined hands as spirit fingers plucked the strings of guitars placed in two ladies' laps. The favor was soon reciprocated when two dozen friends of Mrs. Cushman were entertained at a picnic near Spot Pond in Stoneham.

But by far, the most famous spiritualist in town was Mrs. Fannie Allyn, who began her career as a trance lecturer and the writer of improvisational poetry. She never abandoned these interests but then went on to explore other fields, such as free thought and the true nature of marriage. In particular, spiritualism inspired her to become a nationally known labor activist.

THE INSPIRATIONAL REFORMER: C. FANNIE ALLYN (1841–1927)

Fannie Sampson, born in 1841, had grown up in Middleborough near Plymouth, where her father, Obediah, was a shoemaker. One of her schoolmates, Lavinia Warren Bump (Mrs. Tom Thumb), became her life-long friend. In the early 1860s, her hometown and neighboring communities, such as J. Frank Baxter's Plymouth, were weighing the validity of spiritualism. The *Middleborough Gazette* in May 1863 mentioned that a Mrs. Tabor, a trance medium from Maine, was very disappointing. The editor wryly commented, "Somehow we Plympton folks don't appreciate this kind of inspiration, yet, we are informed that Spiritualism is increasing—Yea, verily."

Fannie married "Reverend" J. Madison Allen from East Bridgewater in 1862. A striking and rather nervous young man, he was an uncompromising vegetarian by choice and an inspirational speaker by profession. Their one son, Lovernest, who arrived a year later, quickly became the center of Fannie's life. By 1866, the couple was advertised in the December 15 issue of the *Banner* as trance speakers on the lecture circuit in New Hampshire.

In 1869, Fannie reinvented herself because her relationship with her husband was in tatters. There were three responses to the event. Her dissatisfied spouse delivered a public sermon on the premise that anyone who married had the right to *un*marry. Looking for a fresh start, the Sampsons, Fannie's parents, brought Lovernest and his mother to Stoneham, where they found a nice location on Hancock Street. And, most important of all, Mrs. Allen changed her name and became C. Fannie Allyn. Within a few weeks, in keeping with her new persona, she delivered trance lectures in New York City, where her bloomer costume of chameleon silk caught the attention of a *New York Herald* reporter in April. The bloomer outfit, since its debut in 1851, featured a knee-length skirt over trousers that were gathered at the ankle. It still symbolized reform and women's rights.

Over the next ten years, Edward Whittier and then his sons published letters from Fannie as she crisscrossed the country speaking about justice for women and the power of spiritualism. She was unafraid to travel alone, not only in the East but also to Texas, where she was one of the first women to address a public gathering. She focused on intellectually stimulating subjects, such as the role of charity and the effects of anger and hatred. Fannie saw herself as a medium but did not engage in the business of holding séances.

On November 1, 1879, Lovernest was suddenly transported into the spirit world, having been ill for a few weeks with typhoid fever. Having come to

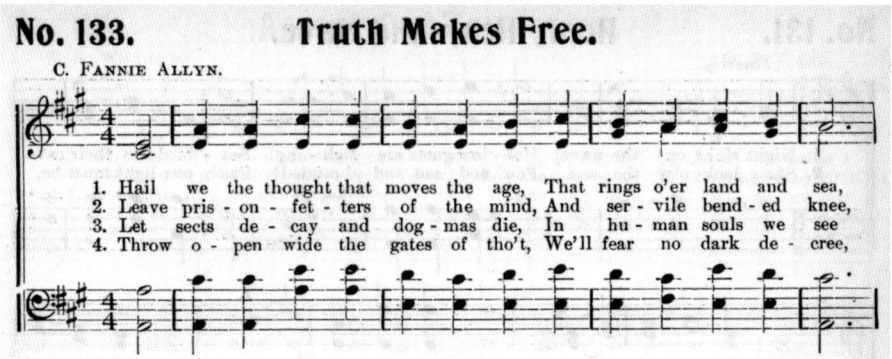

Fannie Allyn, a spiritualist and labor reformer, enjoyed setting words to music. Her hymns were sung at camp meetings. *Author's collection.*

Stoneham as a young boy, he had attended the public high school and was an outstanding member of the Children's Lyceum, a spiritualist version of Sunday school. His mother had just arranged for him to be an intern in a Boston law office. The funeral took place at the Christian Union Church, formerly Unitarian. Lizzie Doten, a Boston medium, was invited to speak because Fannie was not up to the task. On November 15, Mrs. Allyn wrote a brief editorial for the *Independent* expressing her thanks for the good wishes from his classmates and her belief in his eternal future.

The Catalyst and Leader

Living with the experience of her personal loss, Fannie started to counsel believers who were about to make the transition from earth to their spirit homes. Today she would be described as a care provider who visits shut-ins or the terminally ill in order to bring them comfort, as well as assistance in settling their affairs. As part of her outreach, she officiated at funeral services in which she offered moving testimonials about the spiritual outlooks of the departed. Mr. Orne, for example, was noted for his intention to be mindful in eternity of his earthly family. This must have been pleasing to his son, who was a professional clairvoyant in Lynn. Before she "passed upward" in 1883, Mrs. Rosenah Prime had confided to Fannie that death had no power over her because she looked forward to many "sweet hours" of spirit communication with her husband. In addition, she planned her own last rites, which were a dignified celebration of her passage into the world of eternal summer.

During the 1880s, Mrs. Allyn turned to improving conditions for women who labored in factories. She assisted some of the Stoneham shoe workers in forming a cooperative union. Merging separate needs into an organized effort was especially effective in rolling back a wage cut demanded by the Sanborn & Mann Company in 1884. Within three years, she was traveling across America enrolling other workingwomen in unions that were geared toward raising their standard of living.

Fannie became one of the most forceful voices of a new interpretation of spiritualism. Her speech in Boston during a convention in March 1900 was reported by the *Globe* and summed up her vision:

> *We are celebrating one of the great factors in the progress of the universe, the era of mental, spiritual and physical freedom. One of the first things that Spiritualism did was to banish fear of the grave, and next to teach that there was no hell nor heaven but what we make for ourselves. Spiritualism was the first denomination to put woman on the public platform on an equality with man, and to demand that in the same work the pay should be the same. It was the first to announce the power of mind over matter.*

Spiritualism brought a positive dimension to Stoneham. It enjoyed respectability because the editor of the newspaper was a believer. There was a social dimension that encouraged community participation, care for the sick, educational forums and just sheer enjoyment of being together.

Chapter 5
THE TRUTH BEHIND THE ILLUSION

The 1880s introduced a different element into the spiritualist scene because some mediums were highly invested in spectacle. These were the years when fraud was common. Yet it was also the decade when the First Spiritual Temple became a landmark on the Boston scene.

THE DECEPTIVE SIDE OF MEDIUMSHIP: MRS. HANNAH V. ROSS

Charles and Hannah Ross, transplants from Rhode Island, made their Boston debut in February 1881, when they rented part of a house on Davis Street. Since the early days of spiritualism, this neighborhood had attracted mediums and clairvoyant healers, such as Dr. Main, who operated a successful Asylum for the Afflicted. In appearance, Charles was of slighter build than his serious wife, who weighed in at almost two hundred pounds. Often described as genial and accommodating, he was a capable manager in charge of the business side of the séances. Hannah consistently evoked opposing opinions. Her clients were loyal to a fault, writing glowing testimonials whenever needed. E.A. Brackett, of Winchester; A.E. Newton, one of the great pioneers; and John Wetherbee, the dapper stockbroker, never doubted her for a minute. Many newspapers, however, accused her of fraud and reveled in her latest exposé.

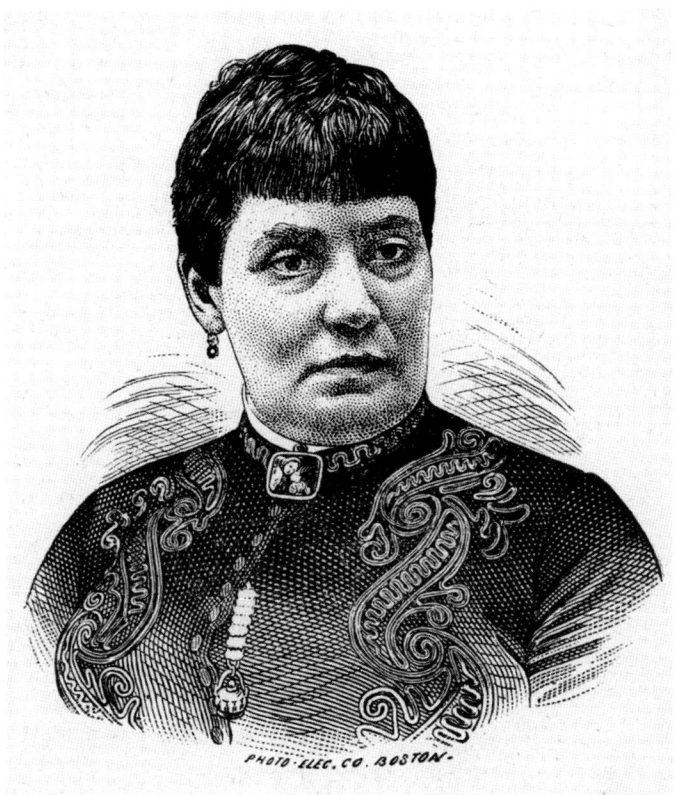

Hannah V. Ross came to Boston with a sketchy past. She was arrested several times for fraud. *Boston Public Library.*

The *Banner of Light* immediately endorsed Mrs. Ross when a veteran sea captain, attending one of her first séances at the recommendation of Luther Colby, recognized one manifestation as his departed wife. Another participant was delighted that the spirits were of different heights and ages, though he wished that they wore more fashionable outfits. After the *Boston Herald* printed a positive review of her performances, the rival *Globe* felt compelled to do its own investigation.

On a cold February night, the *Globe* reporter paid his entrance fee, examined the cabinet draped in thick black cloth and took the last empty seat. He noticed how quiet the audience was when Mr. Ross dimmed the single parlor light prior to winding up a large music box that played popular standards. After leading the group in singing "Home Sweet Home," the host introduced his wife, who was clad in a loose, dark garment that ballooned out over her ample frame. The investigator, a staunch nonbeliever, wondered if there were props concealed beneath the folds. When the gaslight was extinguished, the medium entered the enclosure. A few minutes passed to give her time to become entranced, or so her husband suggested, as he pulled slightly on the front cabinet curtain. Immediately, a steady parade of spirits slowly made their way into the parlor. Some beings shook hands with attendees or exchanged kisses; however, it was difficult to see their features through the semi-transparent face coverings. One lady in the audience thought she recognized her "dear little Mamie" when a fragile spirit child ventured forth briefly. An older man with a grizzled beard responded to several names but was otherwise uncommunicative. Bright Star, the medium's Native American spirit guide, appeared in her fringed doeskin dress and amused everyone by characterizing a gentleman as a "strong brave with no scalp," meaning that he was bald. As part of the finale, another corpulent spirit gently lifted the curtain to reveal Mrs. Ross entirely alone, seated in her chair and in the process of rousing herself from a deep trance. Most of the twenty audience members went home marveling at the experience. The *Globe* correspondent suspected fraud but had no proof. His article, printed a few days later, lambasted Mr. and Mrs. Ross for staging an inferior performance riddled with second-rate effects. He was particularly offended that she was taking advantage of the vulnerable.

Within a few months, the couple left Boston to spend time in Providence, where they owned property. In 1884, an unflattering review of Hannah's séances appeared in the *Providence Daily Journal,* along with a tabloid-worthy description of the couple's early married life. In a spicy interview, Mrs. D.V. Ross, Charles's mother, stated that as a longtime spiritualist, she had supported Hannah's work for years. That changed when she refused to impersonate a spirit in one of her daughter-in-law's performances. Hannah turned her anger toward her husband, scratching him so badly that the police had to be summoned. Emotionally fragile, she deserted Charles briefly when she ran away with her milkman. Husband and wife were reconciled, but Mrs. Daniel Ross was still seething when the *Journal* contacted her. At least that was one side of the story. In the next issue, Hannah published a letter to the editor in which she denied the charges and accused her mother-in-law of maliciously trying to ruin her life.

Luther Colby, expressing outrage over what he termed to be libelous and irresponsible journalism, encouraged the duo to return to Boston. In 1886, their more upscale residence on West Concord Street was open for business. Professor William James of Harvard, a noted investigator of phenomenon, attended a séance based on the gossip that Mrs. Ross had something worthwhile to offer. He was disappointed to see a female figure walk out from the cabinet with her white drapery accidentally caught above her knees. It was clear that she was wearing black trousers, the same type worn by a male spirit who had appeared an instant before. Even more incriminating was the last manifestation. When the form of a very young child materialized and dropped clumsily to the floor, a little boy from the audience ran up to examine the spirit's limp hand. James, leaning forward, realized that it was really a cloth dummy suspended from a cord that stretched around the neck of a short actor dressed in black. The professor's evaluation in the February 19 issue of the *Banner* was scathing: "Whether mediumship was or was not an element of Mrs. Ross's performance, roguery certainly was."

A few businessmen decided that the Ross theatrics had bamboozled the public long enough. Charles Braman, a downtown jeweler, along with John W. Tufts, organist at King's Chapel, were two of the eight who agreed to investigate a few sessions with the intent of carrying out a raid at the first hint of deception. In January 1877, one spirit, looking particularly counterfeit, told Robert McLaughlin that he was a deceased childhood friend. Suspicious, the merchant called out, "Is that you, Harry?" This was the predetermined signal. McLaughlin gripped the form's hand and ripped the gauzy covering off its face. Braman struck several lucifer matches, which illuminated the interior of the cabinet, disclosing a belligerent Mrs. Ross. Braman's son yanked more drapes to the side, just in time to land a blow on a Native American spirit who was threatening him with a raised chair. Mr. Ross was cornered before he could reach for his revolver.

Behind some black curtains that served as a backdrop to the cabinet, the stalwarts found three teenage boys and one trembling eight-year-old girl. She ran crying to Mrs. Ross, who was trying to cover part of the wall with her body. Mr. Braman, pushing the medium aside, removed the mop board that had been partially raised by means of a mechanical device. There in plain sight was a slim but navigable opening abutting a cavity located in the closet of the adjoining room. This was unquestionably the passageway used by the "spirits."

It was not long before Mr. and Mrs. Ross were arrested in mid-February. Lieutenant Walker and Officer James Arbecam, dressed in plainclothes and bearing warrants, attended another séance in the company of a *Post* reporter and some investigators. Confusion reigned when one of the men seized a spirit and carried her kicking and flaying across the room. Mr. Ross fought like a wild animal as furniture was overturned and women screamed. Hannah was apprehended in the cabinet, partially disrobed and in the process of assuming male attire. A sympathetic lady from the audience brought her upstairs to help her get dressed. Meanwhile, a chastened Charlie Ross was offering to refund the entrance fee. The two were escorted to the neighborhood police station but were released on $300 bail each.

Facing charges of fraudulently obtaining money by means of cards, gambling or other tricks, Hannah and Charles faced Judge Parmenter in April 1887. Witnesses for both sides offered conflicting stories about what went on at West Concord Street. The judge was fascinated to learn that Mr. Ross had said, "You have uncovered us, what more do you want?" In the end, Mrs. Ross escaped punishment because the judge decided that séances did not fall under the category of games of chance. Her husband could have faced thirty days in jail but was found not guilty on a technicality. They were marginally vindicated but not declared innocent. Despite having the unwavering support of some spiritualists, Hannah and Charles never regained the status they once held in the Boston community.

Two Mediums and One Entrepreneur: The Berry Sisters and George T. Albro

Helen and Gertrude Berry, Boston born and raised, came from a middle-class background that taught them to capitalize on every opportunity. Because their father had not provided much emotional support since the death of his wife in 1874, the girls struck out on their own in 1880. They moved in with two aunts who owned a boardinghouse at the corner of Arnold and Washington Streets in the upper South End. Helen, an outgoing twenty-three-year-old, quickly found a job in a printing shop, while Gertrude, a few years younger, worked in a bakery. One tenant of the boardinghouse, George T. Albro, managed a sewing machine emporium in the downtown business district where he also did repairs. A twice-married Civil War veteran, this native of Rhode Island was always looking for the next profitable venue. The Berry sisters and the salesman with the handlebar mustache soon learned how much they had in common. The trio formed a business partnership that fulfilled their personal ambitions at the same time that they exploited the good will of many who believed in spiritualism.

It took months of preparation, but by the end of 1882, they were ready to launch their new endeavor. Presenting herself as a professional medium, Helen was eager to produce physical manifestations in which spirits manipulated physical objects as proof of their presence. Albro played the

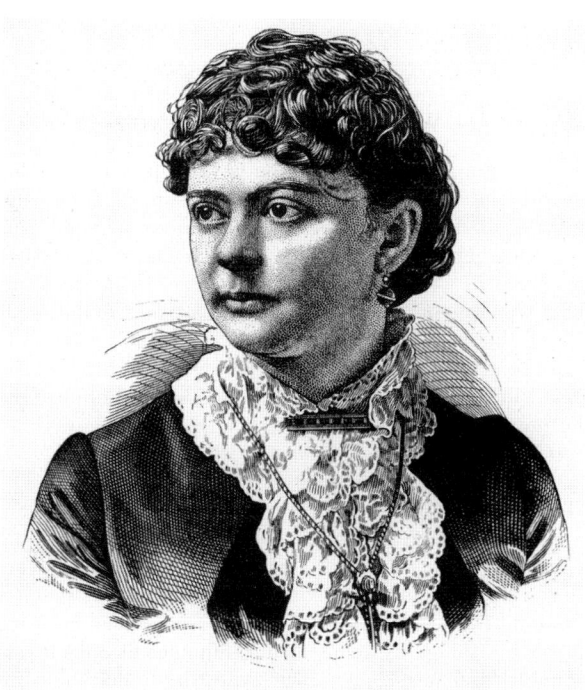

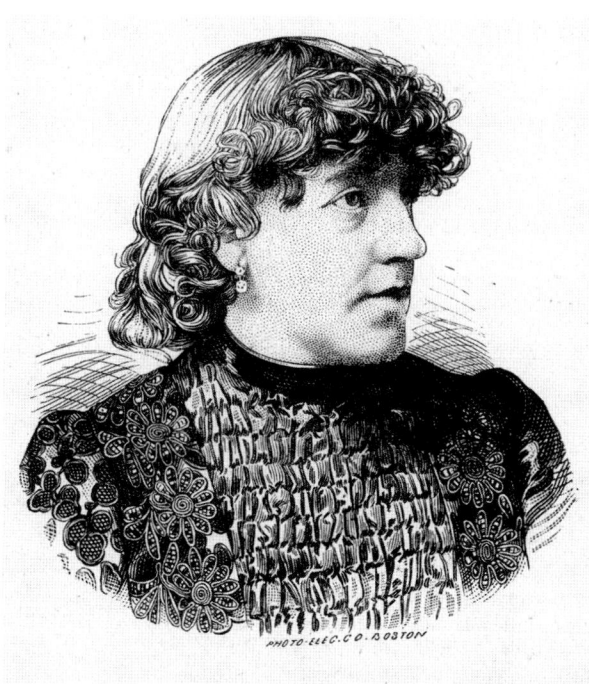

Top: Helen Berry learned to incorporate unusual musical instruments into her act. *Boston Public Library.*

Left: Gertrude Berry was charming and social, which helped her business. *Boston Public Library.*

role of host in charge of the lights. Gertie stayed behind the scenes to assist. An invitation to a séance went out in January 1883 to James L. Ditson, the brother of the famous music publisher, and three friends who were open to communing with the beyond. Ditson's testimonial, published in the *Banner of Light*, praised the simple performance.

In his opinion, the event was conducted with great propriety, even though Mr. Albro had insisted on keeping the parlor very dimly lit. After everyone joined hands around a central table, Helen instructed them to focus on three goblets of water that had been placed in the middle. Two glasses were almost immediately drained, but no one saw how it was done. The third vessel, rising slowly, touched the lips of James, Dr. Moore, Professor Withington and his wife. A remaining piece of ice was gently placed in the mouth of the person next to the medium. Someone in the group whispered that he felt the warmth of a hand close to his head. Another demonstration involved the ringing of bells in different parts of the room. These actions most likely were performed by Gertrude, enveloped in black fabric.

By end of that year, Ditson had witnessed a great expansion of Helen's repertoire. He was captivated as an autophone, a musical instrument that created sound without the use of strings, floated in the near darkness above the sixteen guests who were assembled around a long table. Mr. Albro, clearing his throat in the gloom, reminded the audience that if anyone's chair was slid out from under, that was a signal the spirits were going to lift that person. James's chair was removed on cue and passed over his head to the top of the table while a pair of unseen hands attempted to raise him to it. Unfortunately, because the spirits had not counted on the slipperiness of the smooth surface, Ditson had to steady himself to avoid being dumped on the rug. Helen kept her composure as she reached the dramatic ending. Unseen scribes commandeered blocks of stacked paper. Page after page was torn away, scribbled upon and thrown against the spectators' joined hands. The participants were amazed to find at the end of the program that the room was littered with over three dozen messages written in different penmanship. After many more afternoons spent showcasing Helen, it was time for Gertrude to take the stage.

This Miss Berry was a striking, golden-haired beauty with a fine complexion. Albro liked her gracious way of putting customers at ease. She had learned much from Helen but wanted to develop her own brand of full-form materialization, which necessitated using a wooden cabinet covered with curtains. After she reclined on a couch inside the structure, various beings sallied forth to engage the audience. The male immortals were often suited in black, which nicely offset

The Truth Behind the Illusion

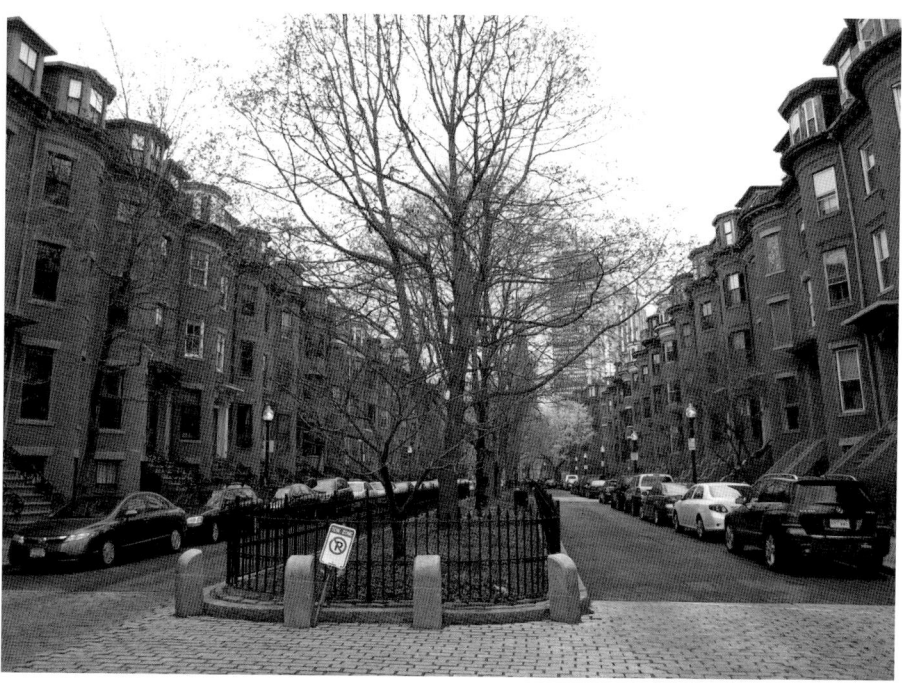

The Berry sisters enjoyed life in the South End, where the clients were well off. The area was a favorite location in which to hold séances. *Ryan Hayward.*

the pure white favored by females. As the shadowy forms approached the guests, cries of "dear mother," "precious husband" or "sweet sister" would ripple through the chamber. By 1884, Gertrude had married to a Mr. E.T. Thompson from Rhode Island, who joined their household. She retained her own name in order to not compromise her popularity. Her spirit control was an unidentified male friend who had passed away young. Helen, in the meantime, had become engaged, but her fiancé, Charley, died shortly before the wedding. She decided to use him as her spirit guide, which added a layer of pathos to her performance.

Business was so brisk in 1885 that the entrepreneurs chose to fit up a house on Rutland Street in the trendy part of the South End. Albro built a wooden cabinet about six feet square that could be rolled into any part of the room. During this chapter of their presentations, Helen and Gertrude practiced physical materialization almost exclusively because their more sophisticated clients wanted to be entertained as well as edified. The women also alternated being the medium on duty, thus leaving one sister to sit in the audience if she desired. It was also a convenient way to eavesdrop on conversations.

Mrs. Marryat, a visiting British novelist, could not help but notice that these Americans attracted a superior class of patrons. A quick glance at the expensive wraps left in the cloakroom confirmed her impression. She was equally ready to point out that the sisters were well educated and that Mr. "Abrow" was one of the most courteous gentlemen she had ever met. In her diary about her trip to the United States, called *There Is No Death*, she acknowledged that she was completely won over when her deceased daughter, Florence, seemed to bound out from the cabinet. The spirit child was clad in a lace and muslin dress that accentuated the silky richness of her waist-length hair. In her arms, she carried twenty damask roses that would have fetched a great deal of money on earth. The being joyfully explained that "Summer Land" was bursting with fields of expensive flowers. With tears streaming down her face, the Englishwoman dropped all her reserve when she explained that the beautiful apparition represented her infant who had died many years ago. This "Florence" was proof that the ten-day-old baby had matured during her time in eternity. Given that revelation, it was anticlimactic when two final forms closed out the session. One was a graceful Asian dancer who swayed provocatively, and the other, dressed in buckskin, announced that he wanted to be friends with the "palefaces." Thus ended another wondrous séance manufactured by the Misses Berry and their colleagues.

Contrasting Views

The *Banner of Light* always spread a protective wing over the Berry sisters. In a torrent of complimentary editorials, it gave an unconditional stamp of approval to every materialization the women generated. It was customary for Colby to urge friends such as Charles G. Foster, a businessman from the West, to attend their productions before returning home. Where else could someone greet an immortal whose handshake seemed to be solid flesh and bone? Luther himself was particularly moved when on one occasion he was summoned to stand in front of the cabinet, the circle being run by Gertrude, to exchange pleasantries with a mystery spirit. Mrs. J.H. Conant, the departed medium of the *Banner*, appeared and folded him in a warm embrace. Although not resembling Fanny, this being assured him that she was often by his side in the office and was as deeply interested in the paper as when she was involved in the Public Circles. The Berry sisters had learned that it was essential to supply immortals with scripts that could not be misinterpreted.

The two mediums fared less well in the secular press. One piece in the *Boston Globe* of May 1885 was an indictment brought about by chance. A young man who was a frequent attendee at Helen's séances came too late to be admitted. Mr. Albro was adamant about closing the front door precisely at eight o'clock. The disappointed gentleman noticed a light on in the room directly above the séance chamber. He crossed the street and prevailed upon the homeowner to allow him access to his roof. That done, he had an unobstructed view into the Berry house. He saw Gertrude arranging her hair and applying makeup for some type of character part. The next evening, he returned to the same vantage point with a reporter. They observed people in white or dark colors walking about, adjusting veils or reading what might have been preparatory notes. The newspaperman had a scoop that caused a great deal of anxiety in the Rutland Street household.

The Albro Cure-All

George T. Albro was grateful to receive the wholehearted endorsement of Luther Colby for more than a dozen years. Besides managing the sisters, he concocted medicines and devices. One of his most successful efforts, Albro's Magnetized Paper, was invented to convey "the essence of life." These small expensive sheets saturated with "electrical and magnetic currents" were sold in packets. A customer was instructed to hold the treated paper in both hands for ten to fifteen minutes, occasionally passing it across her forehead. After the magnetic force was imparted, the sheet was to be placed nearby. Two main results were possible. Diseases such as sciatic rheumatism could be cured. Or, if inclined, a buyer might access her clairvoyant powers. Marketing this product and others gave Albro some independence.

A more elaborate procedure was available to those who wanted to pay more. For an extra dollar per session, a client, holding magnetized paper, could sit inside a séance cabinet with Dr. Albro by her side. Following his prompts, the medium-in-training focused on contacting departed loved ones. If he were not available, his assistant, "Harry," would substitute. All was well until the operation hit a real snag in 1886. It happened that a Mrs. S. from Haverhill had spent a great sum of money but had achieved very little. There was something that bothered her when she was obliged to deal with "Harry" in that he sometimes got too familiar. Then there was something about his voice. Had she heard it before? Months later, when speaking with Mr. Thompson, Gertrude Berry's husband, she made the sudden connection. There was no doubt in her mind that "Harry" and this man were one and the same person. Her belief in spiritualism disintegrated. By 1889, she was a witness against Albro when he was tried for fraud.

The Creator of the First Spiritual Temple: Marcellus S. Ayer (circa 1840–1921)

The First Spiritual Temple, costing over $250,000, was built on the corner of Exeter and Newbury Streets, one of the most desirable lots in Copley Square. Designed by the prestigious Devonshire Street firm of Hartwell & Richardson, the Romanesque-style edifice combined elegance and utility. Two wide flights of stairs led from the vestibule to a grand auditorium with a gallery, organ loft and speakers' platform. Stained-glass windows bathed 1,500 chairs in soft light, while on the next floor there were seven large lecture suites, a kitchen, janitor's quarters and smaller rooms. The huge ventilating chamber in a portion of the third level housed the ducts that supplied fresh air. From the Newbury Street side, a stairway led down to the basement, which contained a lyceum or conservatory hall for the instruction of children. A generous space was reserved for a library and reading room with enough left over to include a ticket office and a meeting room for the officers of the corporation. At the request of the spirits, all the services were free and open to everyone.

This was the magnificent gift of a wealthy wholesale grocer who funded the entire project with his own fortune. He was respected within the community but relatively unknown. People knew that he had gone from a blue-collar existence in the 1860s to living in an elegant mansion on West Chester Park ten years later. His small shop on Blackstone Street was the steppingstone to an emporium in the business district. Along the way, he had embraced spiritualism.

Ayer had been turning over the idea of building an elegant house of worship for years. He remembered when *Facts* magazine, in March 1876, had criticized some self-absorbed spiritualists for not providing the necessary funds. By 1881, he was ready to take on the challenge. He established the Working Union of Progressive Spiritualists, a society dedicated to advancing members to a higher plane of knowledge. This band of altruistic believers

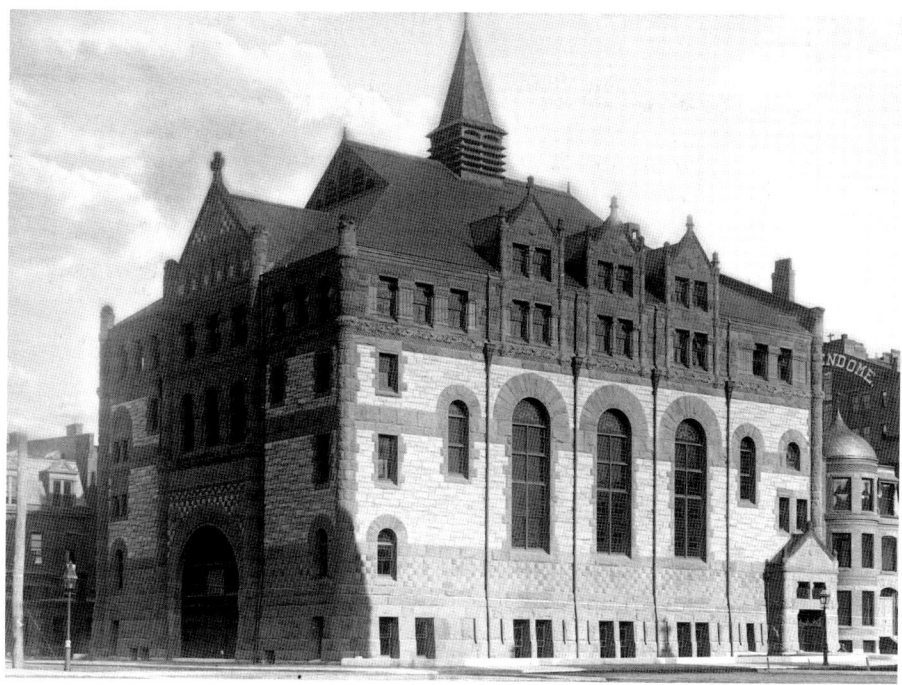

The stunning First Spiritual Temple on Exeter Street was primarily the gift of one man, Marcellus S. Ayer. *Boston Public Library.*

formed the core of a committee intent on erecting the edifice. Every week for months, the union members and other interested parties attended services at the Ayer home, followed by strategy meetings. Hattie supplied organ music, while Marcellus led the meeting in which notables such as Isabella Beecher Hooker presented their ideas.

On a fine weekend in September 1885, the First Spiritual Temple was dedicated. Many spirits attended, along with earthly delegations from across the city. The speaker's platform, decorated in autumnal fruit, held a quartet and Mrs. Dyer, a trance medium who spoke about the future. A number of guests were members of other congregations and were attending out of curiosity. It was a brilliantly successful event.

THE FIRST PASTOR OF THE TEMPLE: MRS. HENRY S. LAKE

Sarah Genevra Chafa always created a sensation because people knew that in the 1870s, she had married Father Henry S. Lake, a young Catholic priest from New York. They had met about 1864 at a charity event staged by an amateur theater group they both supported. Coming from a wealthy Protestant family, he served in a Lower Manhattan parish, where he preached on temperance and the public schools. She, having suffered numerous misfortunes, was a budding poet who boarded with a wealthy suffragette. Although Father Lake struggled between allegiance to his vows and his love for the pretty brunette, Sarah overcame his scruples. They were secretly married in 1874, living under the name of Edmonds, yet were still the target of persecution. The star-crossed couple fled to California, where they found happiness but little employment in Santa Cruz. Less than two years later, the handsome ex-cleric died from consumption, thus leaving his destitute wife to survive on her own. Resilient but angry, Sarah billed herself as the "Widow of Father Lake" in her new career as an anti-Catholic lecturer. By 1877, Mrs. H.S. Lake, now a professional medium inspired by her spirit husband, was traveling throughout the West. Her life moved in a new direction when she began a relationship with Professor William F. Peck, a spiritualist in the process of a divorce. Her distaste for marriage prompted her to draw up a contract describing the two as co-partners living together as long as love survived.

Mr. Peck and Mrs. Lake joined the Boston community by 1884. The Office of the Working Union of Progressive Spiritualists, just down the street on Columbus Avenue, was actively canvassing for volunteers to do some fundraising. It is likely that this was her introduction to Marcellus Ayer and his supporters. Her inspired style, coupled with a progressive outlook, got her a position as an occasional speaker at the temple. She was the official pastor within three years. Her thought-provoking lectures, delivered under spirit guidance, did not require the use of any props or a cabinet. Topics such as "Ireland and the Irish" allowed her to bring to the fore her passion for freedom from constraints. She became active in political issues in the 1890s, such as supporting the rights of homeopathic physicians. Professor Peck kept busy by presenting programs in the suburbs.

In 1891, Mrs. Lake found herself in the Suffolk County Divorce Court. William testified that after thirteen years of being together, Sarah had abruptly deserted him in 1888. The only reason she gave was that her spirit guides urged that it would be to her advantage as well as his. After a long deliberation, Judge

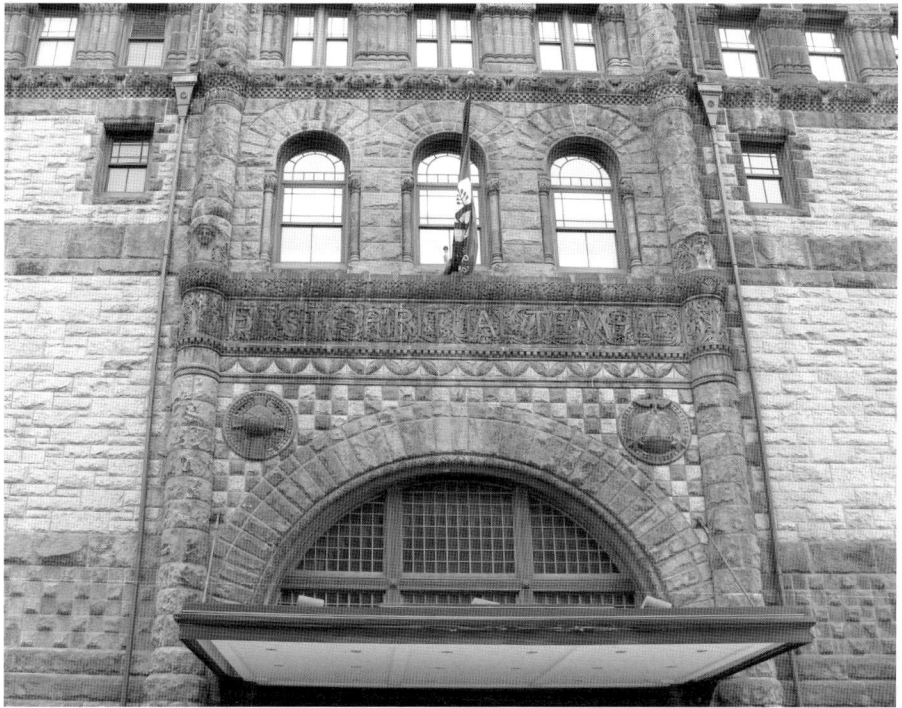

Above the door, the carved "First Spiritual Temple" is an elegant reminder of the building's first use. *Ryan Hayward.*

Staples ruled that he could not grant a divorce since there had never been a marriage. Their contract had stipulated that the couple stay together until the union became disagreeable. Elated, Mrs. Lake prepared a new series of talks with the first one entitled: "Love, Marriage and Divorce." Now living in her own home at West Chester Park, she continued to move forward on women's rights, freedom of speech and true discernment of spirits. Her programs at the Temple attracted progressives as well as believers.

The Mediums Who Were Genuine Fakes: The Concannons from Kansas

Mr. Ayer did not realize that he was in for a huge headache when his spirit guides told him to book Edella and Oliver Concannon, materialization mediums from Kansas. He did promise the Temple faithful that they were in for quite a show one Sunday in November 1896. Setting the mood, Mrs. Ayer sang a few hymns while accompanying herself on the organ. Her husband exhorted the audience to pay close attention to Reverend Mrs. Concannon, who opened the service by gliding about the hall. She pledged that all the messages were from departed spouses and friends. Then Reverend Mr. Concannon made quite a display out of drinking eight glasses of water. Supposedly, his spirit contacts needed the extra fluid to manifest themselves properly. Drawing the drape aside, he entered the cabinet as the lights were lowered. After a bit, a tall figure with long flowing locks and a beard strode forth with manly vigor to speak about the glories of the hereafter. He was followed by a white-robed "female" named the Queen of the Cabinet, who exchanged pleasantries with people in the front rows. After a few others showed their ghostly faces, the audience was shocked to see five men race up to the stage. Three raiders grabbed wigs, several silk robes, a set of whiskers, a lacy cloak and a rubber mask, among other trophies. They ran down the aisle holding their prizes aloft as the hall erupted in confusion and anger. Reverend Mr. Concannon was led upstairs to recuperate. The jubilant young men proceeded to a nearby police station to explain themselves. Meanwhile, a visibly shaken Proprietor Ayer suggested to a *Globe* reporter that the hooligans had concealed the outfits on their persons as part of a premeditated plan. Mrs. Concannon, scarlet with rage, cursed anyone who discredited her husband.

Over the next few days, the story of the raid sent ripples through the Back Bay community. The *Globe* even printed a letter from a Bostonian who stated that he had witnessed the Concannons being debunked during a show in Oklahoma City. By the end of December, the costume-snatchers were facing charges of malicious mischief and disturbing a religious meeting. The defendants testified that they were investigating a fraudulent performance. They admitted that there had been a great deal of kicking and punching committed by everyone, even Mr. Ayer. Their witnesses included the Concannons' landlady, who said that a woman in her house had hand-sewn the robes for the mediums to use in their act. On the other side, Mrs. Concannon went on record to state that she had been struck in the side by one of the gang when he took a gown from under his coat and threw it on the cabinet floor. Judge Forsaith fined the men fifty dollars a piece for disturbing a lawful gathering. Relieved that the episode was finally over, Manager Ayer set about restoring the reputation of the Temple. He was positive that the materializations had been authentic.

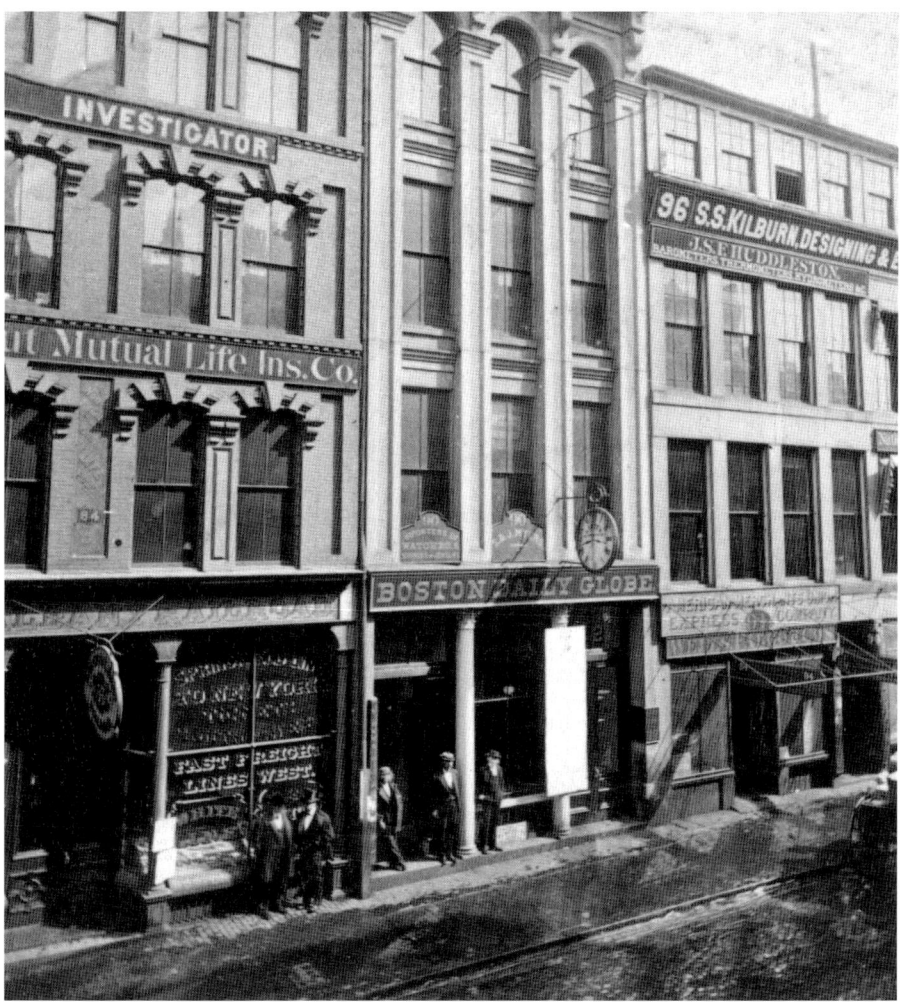

An array of newspapers offered their opinions on spiritualism. The offices of the *Investigator* and the *Boston Globe* were in proximity to each other. *Boston Public Library.*

In 1914, the Temple was converted into a cinema showplace by Mrs. Ayer, who was described as a wealthy socialite. Attendance had continued to decline, but there was space reserved for meetings. Lasting well into the twentieth century in this capacity, the Exeter Street Theatre was known for its art films. It was still owned by the spiritualists.

The Transition of Luther Colby: 1894

The golden leaves of October 1894 marked the entrance into the spirit world of Luther Colby, the gallant old standard bearer of the *Banner of Light*. From its very beginning in 1857 through the financially difficult years of the 1860s and into the more stable times of later decades, Colby had been ever at the helm. As the *Globe* remarked: "To many thousands of his readers, he was prophet and priest, and the utterances of the *Banner* were considered as infallible." He formed a permanent bond with William Berry, his first co-editor, and treated Fanny Conant, the *Banner*'s chief medium, like a cherished sister. Other women were important members of the staff, such as Miss Chase from Somerville, who was a reporter for over fifteen years. He did not hesitate to support better working conditions for women and men laboring in factories and the many sweatshops scattered throughout the city. As editor, he made it a practice to attend the séances of emerging mediums, those new to Boston or even those clairvoyants who had been established for years. Colby felt duty-bound to give his honest opinion on the professionals who working within the Greater Boston community.

During the last twelve years of his life, he lived at the Crawford House, a residential hotel located in Boston's old Scolley Square. Mrs. T.P. Thaxter, the manager, was especially attentive to his needs and cared for him like a dutiful daughter. She even shuttered her own business as a trance medium in order to help him keep up with his correspondence. He kept on file any exchanges with readers, supporters and, more importantly, critics.

Colby was a medium possessing considerable gifts, although he never held séances for friends or subscribers. Many of his contemporaries were unaware that one of his spirit guides was named Ocean Brave, a powerfully built Native American. He often accessed the spirit of Reverend Theodore Parker in order to gain perspective on the social reforms of the day. Other immortals suggested that he print verbatim the sermons of ministers of different faiths as long as the preachers were not hostile to the movement. He received a spirit communication to establish "God's Poor Fund" and other charities that served the less fortunate.

The newspaper was so much part of his existence that he did not find his relaxation in belonging to social clubs or spending time on hobbies. On a rare day, he enjoyed walking along the Chelsea beach followed by spending a few relaxing minutes on the veranda of the summer hotel. His walk to and from the office became a lengthy exercise because he spent time talking with his many acquaintances.

If he had a fault, it was his unwavering trust in the honesty of some mediums who specialized in the dramatic displays of the 1870s and later years. Horace Seaver, his longtime friend and editor of the free-thought newspaper the *Boston Instigator*, criticized his lack of discernment but admired his integrity.

Colby's funeral took place on October 10 at the First Spiritual Temple, the auditorium barely holding his multitude of friends. Moses, his only surviving brother, was given a place of honor. The service was very simple because he disliked elaborate rituals, even though he had endured many of them during his lifetime. He chose to be cremated, a bold move for the times. His passing closed a very large chapter in the story of Boston spiritualism.

The Perfect Manager: Isaac B. Rich (1827–1908)

The formal portrait captured much of the personality of Boston's most famous theater manager. Isaac Baker Rich was every inch a successful businessman who enjoyed posing in a dark suit accented with a gold watch and chain. For half a century, his name was synonymous with quality entertainment presented in an elegant setting. He was decisive yet flexible, a winning combination in a profession dependent on satisfying the whims of the public. His colleagues admired his liberal generosity as much as they marveled at his ability to discover new dramatic talent. Rich came to embrace spiritualism with equal intensity because that was his style. He could not tolerate being neutral.

Isaac's first job as a printer's apprentice taught him about the inner workings of the newspaper business. After learning everything that he could in Bangor, Maine, he moved on to a new adventure in New Orleans, where he sold gallery tickets at the Poydras Street playhouse. He was thrilled when he landed a small role in a Shakespearean tragedy starring Edwin Forrest, the foremost actor of the day. His acting ability was adequate yet unexceptional; however, his instinct to immerse himself in the performing arts was on target. By the 1840s, in his twenties, Rich was back in Boston, where he served as an assistant, among other positions, to the stage director of the National Theatre. His next step up was to begin a revitalization of the Howard Athenaeum, which at one time had been an upscale venue that attracted the likes of Forrest, his early mentor. In the position of manager

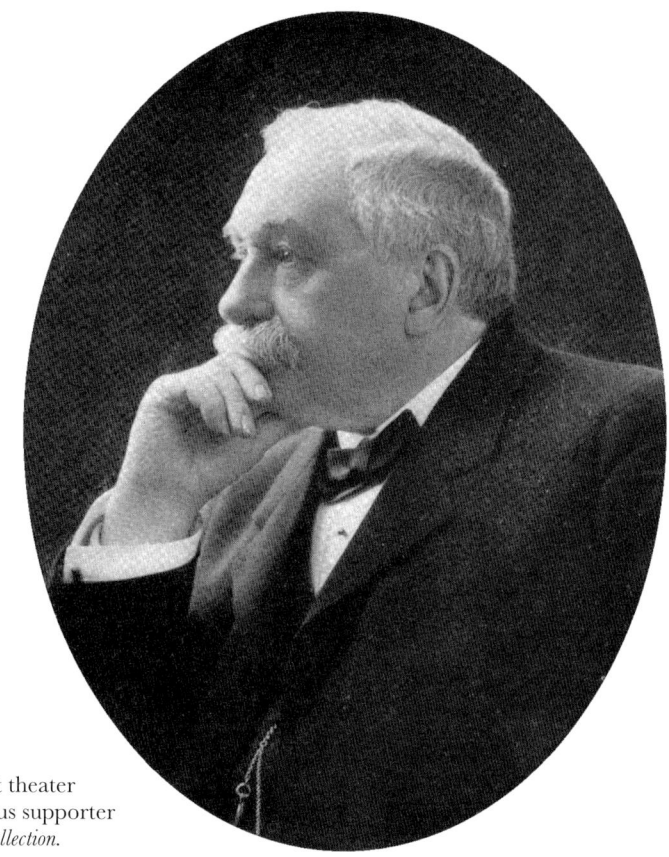

Isaac B. Rich, the great theater manager, was a generous supporter of the *Banner. Author's collection.*

and lessee of the building in 1866, he introduced a new stock company in addition to filling out the orchestra with more musicians. His biggest innovation was launched a few years later when he changed the theater format from traditional drama to the multiple-act variety show. Vaudeville brought in a younger crowd with a little extra money to spread around.

THE GENEROUS SPIRITUALIST

Rich's occasional participation in séances in early 1861 brought him into contact with Luther Colby, who immediately asked for his business help. He became an informal adviser, keeping his distance until the threat of bankruptcy loomed. When the paper abruptly relocated to New York City in an attempt to save itself financially, Isaac stepped forward with an amazing gesture of support. He supplied all the funds necessary to redeem the journal that was the heartbeat of Boston spiritualism. The following announcement in March 1861 gave an understated explanation of the *Banner*'s return to its birthplace: "At the urgent solicitation of friends in Boston, who felt that the *Banner of Light* was needed in New England, and who have held out such pecuniary inducements as are satisfactory to us, we have returned to Boston. We have associated with us a gentleman of well known and tried integrity, and of means, and the business of the *Banner of Light* will be hereafter carried on here."

His generosity continued as he underwrote some "new and commodious rooms" of Washington Street in July. Breaking his silence in print, he emphasized that the *Banner* would "enlighten, refine and elevate society." His long tenure as proprietor, publisher and confidant had begun. Rich's allegiance to spiritualism never wavered, even when his six-year-old son, George, suddenly passed away after a brief illness in 1864. Rich was grounded in his belief that his spirit boy could be contacted through any of the trusted mediums affiliated with the *Banner*.

The Complex Private Man

While Rich's professional history was an open record, his private life was far less known, especially the story of his relationships. After almost eighteen years of being together, Isaac and Elizabeth severed their marital bond. This did not divide the family because their children were entering adulthood and close to becoming independent. At the end of 1870, Isaac married Fanny Marsh, a twenty-four-year-old actress, who was happy to provide a home for Rich's teenage son, Charles. Mrs. Marsh-Rich quickly received prominent billing in the Howard Athenaeum productions and was so well received that she was able to manage her own small theater. Their happiness did not last because Fanny filed for divorce in 1878, accusing Isaac of desertion and failure to provide support. The *Boston Globe* on January 31 published a small article about the two being "theatrical people" while the *Banner* remained tactfully silent. It would have been poor form to criticize Rich when several of the most popular Boston mediums were divorcing and remarrying several times. Many spiritualists did not believe in staying in a loveless marriage.

Within two years, Rich found his soul mate in the person of Mary E. Cale, a young woman sympathetic to his beliefs. Their marriage was cut short in 1885 when she passed to spirit life as the result of weak heart. The *Banner* published a lengthy description of her funeral, which was held at the Revere House, a residential hotel that had been their home. Only thirty-two at the time, she was two decades younger than her grieving spouse, who was left with the care of their young daughter. Symbolic of the spirit's entrance into a better state, the casket was draped in white broadcloth and surrounded by floral displays of lilies. As the January 4 article stated: "The absence of anything sombre in appearance or black in color [was] an emblematic indication of the brighter views inculcated at the grave's edge by the new revelation of the nineteenth century." Mrs. M.T. Shelhamer, the in-house medium of the paper, delivered fitting remarks just before the choir sang "Shall We Meet Beyond the River?" and over one hundred believers paid their respects. Then the body was conveyed to Forest Hills Cemetery in Jamaica Plain, where Mary was interred in the Rich family plot next to George, Isaac's young son. Later in 1885, Rich published a letter in the *Banner* in which he revealed that he had been forewarned of his young wife's untimely passing. He had hired Professor St. Leon, a New York astrologer, to chart her future based on the alignment of the planets. Sadly, the prediction that she would not survive a sudden heart attack had been accurate even to the day and time. Rich continued, nevertheless, to use the professor's services on matters pertaining to business.

Apparently, Isaac was more comfortable being a husband rather than a widower because in 1886 he was united with Pauline Babo, a twenty-eight-year-old woman of good character. This final Mrs. Rich gave birth in 1890 to a son, Ralph, who was a constant source of joy to his devoted father. They lived in a large apartment in the Hotel Buckminster, which was not far from the theaters.

The Public Showman

During these successive marriages, Rich went forward with more extravagant business projects. At the end of 1885, his friend Luther Colby wrote a long piece congratulating his partner on opening one of the most beautiful playhouses ever to be constructed in Boston. The Hollis Street Theatre, designed by Colonel John R. Hall, was a triumph of pastel walls, gilt-edged

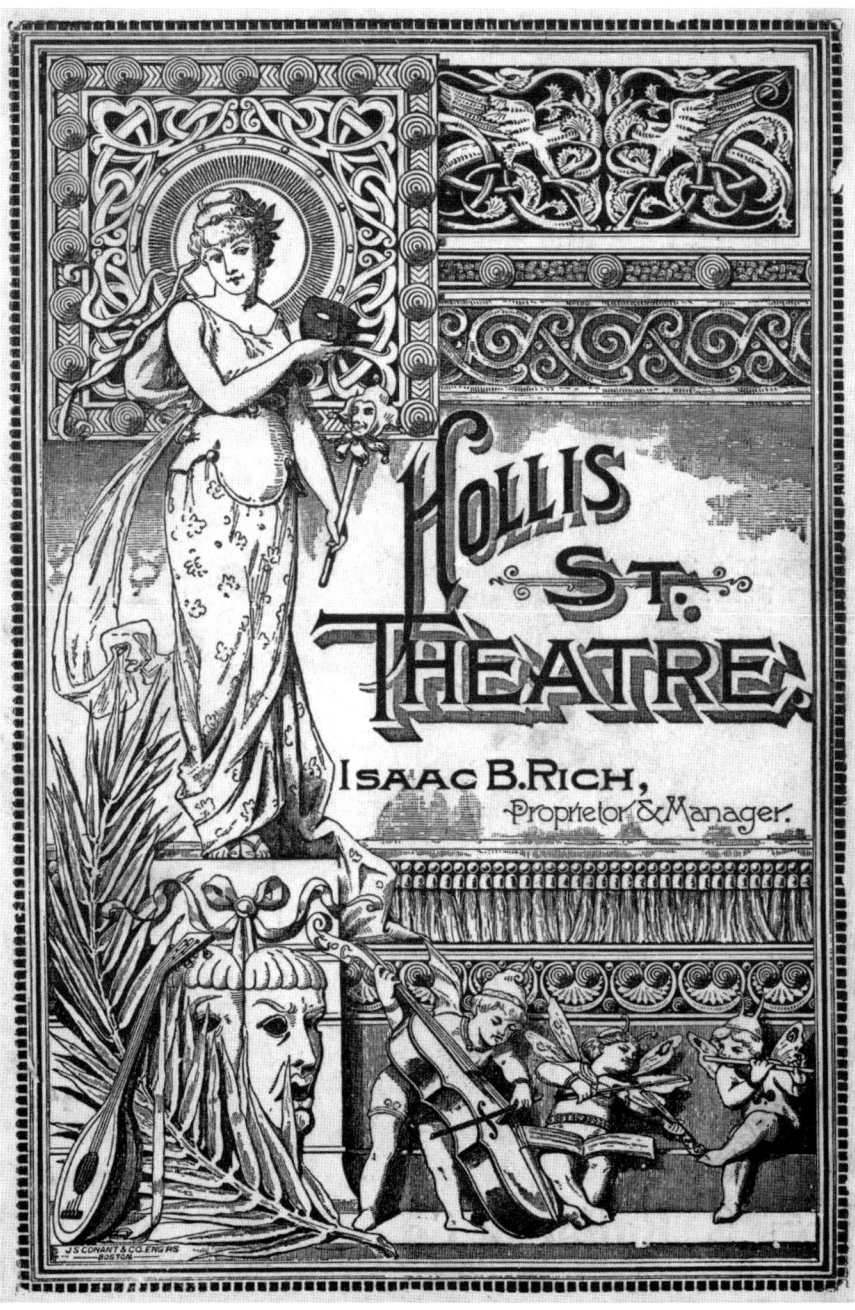

The Hollis Street Theatre was one of the most elegant entertainment palaces in Boston. It was built on the site where John Pierpont preached. *Author's collection.*

balconies and crystal chandeliers. Of great significance was the symbolic value of the site. This magnificent edifice had risen from the ashes of the Hollis Street Church, whose congregation had fought with Reverend John Pierpont during the early days of his ministry. Pierpont, an ardent spiritualist, was now in spirit life and a frequent visitor to the Public Circles. Isaac was proud to mention that important connection when he composed a poem to be read at the dedication. His adult son, Charles, formerly a clerk in Colby's office, became the assistant manager whose first duty was to superintend the evening's festivities on November 11. There were occasions when the *Banner* staff was provided with complimentary tickets to attend performances. During the 1890s, Manager Rich would go on to operate the Columbia, Bowdoin Square and Park Theatres. The Colonial, still in business today on Boylston Street, was Rich's last addition to Boston's theater district.

Boston mourned Isaac B. Rich in numerous obituaries that praised his accomplishment of transforming simple wooden theaters into architectural jewels. The June 11, 1908 *Globe* noted that "with his death the older school of theatrical managers becomes extinct." Meanwhile, the spiritualist community rejoiced that their longtime benefactor had passed to the world beyond in which he was connecting again with his associates from the early days of financial struggle. His last rites were a welcome to heaven rather than a farewell to earth.

A Shared Business and a Different View

Isaac B, Rich, the manager, and Harry Houdini, the performer, loved entertaining the public with all the spectacle, movement and color that was at the heart of vaudeville. Both believed that the customer deserved a fair return for his money and the opportunity to be lifted out of the boredom of daily routine. Rich earned his fortune behind the scenes while Houdini became wealthy enjoying every moment in the limelight. Spiritualism also factored in both their lives, but the results were opposite. Isaac had faith and gained insights into the next world. Harry was a vocal antagonist, determined to expose fraudulent mediums.

THE ILLUSIONIST WHO HATED DECEPTION: HARRY HOUDINI (1874–1926)

Houdini said that he was from Appleton, Wisconsin. In reality, he was born in Hungary with the name Erich Weisz. His father, a rabbi, brought the family to America and the Fox River Valley in the Midwest. In the late 1880s, they were coping with urban life in New York, where Erich was soon completely fascinated with show business. He changed his name to Houdini, a gesture to Houdin, a celebrated French magician, and quickly gained notoriety for his ability to escape from handcuffs. By 1899, he was performing with such audacity that he was a major celebrity in the expanding world of vaudeville.

Harry always chose B.F. Keith's entertainment palace as his major venue when visiting the Hub. This elegant shrine to the variety show was a landmark in the theater district. Thomas Edison had demonstrated the Viatascope projector there in 1894, marking the first time that local audiences were treated to a movie. All seats were reserved by purchasing a ticket at one of the two box offices. The window fronting Tremont Street opened at 6:00 p.m. and was visible to pedestrians walking in Boston Common. The other, opening at 2:00 p.m., caught the eye of shoppers hurrying along the Washington Street corridor. Performances began in the early afternoon and ran continuously until late in the evening. People came in at any time and remained until the act they had seen first came round again.

Houdini arrived in town for an extended stay in February 1906. The *Globe* suggested that anyone interested in a little fun should bring to the show a set of handcuffs, especially the kind with "new fangled locks and keys." Members of the audience came equipped, but attempts to outsmart the escape artist failed. At the close of his set, Harry reminded them that there were few mysteries that could not be solved by close observation. The remainder of the evening included a silent film about moose hunting in Canada and the four Colinis, Parisian acrobatic dancers. These paled in comparison to the mystery that was Houdini.

Billed as "The Single Greatest Attraction Vaudeville Has Ever Known," Harry was featured in the January 1907 *Globe* entertainment section, directly above the ad for the Hollis Street Theatre, managed by the veteran Mr. Rich. Houdini headlined a varied program of fifteen acts with something for every taste, even those interested in Frank Bush, the storyteller. Drawing a full house twice a day, Harry exhibited his new achievements. He escaped from a closely woven wicker hamper girded with iron bands in the record time of sixty-two minutes. A few days later, he took under half an hour to free himself from a padlocked leather mail pouch surrounded with steel chains. He asked the public to send him challenges. If there was a way to stump him, he wanted to hear about it. Boston audiences could not get enough of Houdini's exploits.

One month before Isaac B. Rich passed into the spirit world in 1908, Houdini pulled off one of his most daring feats. On May 1, thousands of men, women and children crowded onto and around the Harvard Bridge, a major span connecting Boston and Cambridge, where they waited to see if Harry could cheat death one more time. Always trying to outdo himself, he was tightly manacled and wound about with chains. Then, as the spectators fell silent, the physically fit but wild-looking man dramatically jumped into the cold waters of the Charles River. Time crept by as spectators looked increasingly grim. Suddenly, having divested himself of his weighty shackles, Harry's head broke through the light waves to be greeted with sustained cheers.

Today, over one hundred years later, a plaque commemorates the event: "In memoriam to the great Artist and Past National President who performed one of his well-known escapes from this bridge on May 1, 1908." Placed there by the Society of American Magicians in 1994, it is a tribute to Houdini's skill as a fearless illusionist. Boston has also not forgotten his investigations in the field of spiritualism.

Doyle, Houdini and Investigations

Before the 1920s, Sir Arthur Conan Doyle, the creator of Sherlock Holmes, had become a fervent believer in spirit communication. The death of his son during World War I provided the impetus for him to frequent mediums and thus receive the consolation he craved. Houdini, having experienced the loss of his mother, had also experimented with séances, but his powers of observation and innate skepticism dismissed the events as counterfeit. When the mystery writer made Harry's acquaintance in England, the two became friends based on their mutual curiosity about the afterlife. Sir Arthur realized that not every clairvoyant was honest but hesitated to engage in exposés. They maintained a correspondence and, in general, agreed to disagree.

Their bond began to erode in 1924, when Harry published *A Magician Among the Spirits*. He found that "trifling with the hallowed reverence which the average human being bestows on the departed" was not only frivolous but also close to being criminal. Sir Arthur was quoted as encouraging the seeker to continue investigating despite setbacks. Harry answered emphatically: "I am further along than ever from belief in the genuineness of Spirit manifestations and after twenty-five years of ardent research and endeavor I declare that nothing has been revealed to convince me that intercommunication had been established."

In that same year, the *Scientific American Magazine* offered two handsome cash rewards for a genuine spirit photograph or the verification of a spirit presence. Somewhat reminiscent of the Harvard Investigation of 1857, an impartial committee was formed to evaluate any entries. Houdini was one of the investigators, along with others who represented both sides of the argument, such as William McDougall, a Harvard psychologist, and Hereward Carrington, an amateur magician and independent researcher of the paranormal. Mina "Margery" Crandon, presented herself as the candidate endorsed by Arthur Conan Doyle. Her credibility was enhanced when she declared her intention to donate the prize to charity if she won.

Blond, attractive and thirty-six years old, Margery was already known for the séances she held at her home on Boston's Lime Street. Her wealthy, much older and Harvard-connected husband, Dr. LeRoi Crandon, believed in her powers as well as his own psychic strengths. During some meetings, she extruded from her mouth, nose or ears a slithery substance called ectoplasm, which was supposed to be the external manifestation of spiritual energy. It was reported that she often appeared in the nude. Her spirit guide was her deceased brother, Walter, who had a tendency to become irritable.

Over the course of many sessions before the investigating committee, Margery's tests included the traditional phenomena of the spontaneous movement of objects—unique to this case was a "flying' megaphone"—and the touch of invisible hands. Her husband also participated as a show of his support, making sure to sit next to his wife. The sittings produced mixed opinions, with Carrington being the only one definitely certain that she was genuine. Houdini, having been absent during some of the proceedings, returned in time to attend some of Margery's private séances. He became convinced that she was one of the most complete examples of fraud that he had ever encountered.

At the beginning of 1925, Harry, now a professor at a new school for police detectives in New York, gave a series of demonstrations in which he showed the students how fake mediums confused the audience. Then he performed the illusions in slow motion. Coming back to Boston, he brought the lectures to Keith's Theatre in May in order to enlighten the ministers of the city and highlight more of Margery's tricks. An unidentified woman stood up and accused him of "working against the science and knowledge of the future." By the summer, Boston detectives had initiated their own type of dramatics by launching a campaign to crack down on the numerous charlatans posing as legitimate psychics. Scores were arrested, particularly those who were working out of questionable locations in the South End. In December, the *Scientific American*'s committee returned its decision that Mrs. Crandon had failed to produce valid examples of psychic manifestations. Four members of the panel, including Houdini, had voted in the negative.

A month later, the papers announced that Houdini was considering legal action against Sir Arthur for some "harsh remarks" made against him because of Margery's exposé. The public feud between the two former friends was exacerbated when Harry issued his uncompromising pamphlet titled *Houdini Exposes the Tricks Used by the Boston Medium, "Margery."* He later incorporated into his stage act some of the sleight-of-hand tricks that he had observed her performing. One minor one involved using a concealed ruler to ring a suspended bell. Houdini's public appearances were fueled by his determination to bring fraud to the attention of the public.

Margery and her husband returned to Lime Street to continue her séances for people who believed in her powers. Reportedly, she was not unhappy when Houdini died less than a year later, in 1926, from a fatal infection. His relentless negative publicity had made inroads on her business. After Sir Arthur passed away in 1930, Mrs. Crandon indicated that he was a frequent spirit presence in her home. Over time, her health was compromised, and her séances became very infrequent. Her name continued to be remembered in conjunction with the *Scientific American* challenge. Margery entered eternity in 1941. Her remains were interred in the family plot at Forest Hills Cemetery, the final resting place of so many pioneers in Boston spiritualism.

EPILOGUE

Even before Houdini's campaign to expose the fraud was in full gear, newspapers were examining the illusions practiced by flashy performers working in large venues. On December 5, 1896, the *Boston Globe* ran an article using an "ex medium" as its source. The former "clairvoyant" admitted that he and many of his colleagues were showmen without any ties to spiritualism. To avoid entanglements with the law, they made their position clear at the beginning of each show: "We will not claim that any of the manifestations are the workings of disembodied spirits, neither will we deny it." The visual extravaganzas depended on a trapdoor connecting the stage with a cavity where "spirits" were concealed. Other "spirit sightings" were achieved by producing images reflected in well-polished sheets of glass that were carefully positioned so as to be invisible to the audience. The apparent changing of one substance into another occurred, for example, by leaving a few drops of iodine at the bottom of a glass. When water was poured in, the liquid was immediately "converted" into port wine. The acts depended on concealed hooks, imperfectly tied ropes and assistance from a crew of stagehands.

Many houses used in private séances were found to contain hollowed-out walls, sliding panels and the customary trapdoor. The Berry sisters and Hannah Ross were very reluctant to hold séances in unfamiliar settings because the effects could not be easily controlled. The hunger for "display" had become more important than content.

For years, other mediums had collected information by reading obituaries and seeking out dates, family connections and causes of death written in city records or by chatting up the friends of clients. Sometimes the knowledge was pooled during popular events such as camp meetings. Many practitioners kept extensive notebooks. Frank Baxter was one of the most zealous recorders.

Meanwhile, the pioneers and their immediate successors were continuing to leave the public arena. The Union of Veteran Spiritualists bought a retirement home at Waverley Oaks in the suburbs in the 1890s. There was a push to provide food and clothing for mediums who were needy. Believers attending conventions were cautioned to be careful of any new psychic who seemed out for personal gain. People were connecting to new technology whereby they conversed with "disembodied" voices via the telephone.

On the positive side, spiritualism rested on the premise that death had been conquered. This epiphany transformed the lives of the grieving. It resonated in the groves of Forest Hills Cemetery, where many monuments proclaimed that the departed, in passing to a higher life, had not severed bonds with those left behind.

Women involved in the movement were able to offer their opinions as well as become more proactive in society. They could earn livings as lecturers, take on other reforms or perhaps redefine their relationships. Men benefited from the focus on healthy introspection and the exploration of challenges outside their comfort zones.

It was appropriate that spiritualism took root in Boston and flourished. John Wetherbee, a stockbroker who consulted mediums about business opportunities and an ardent spiritualist himself, wrote in his 1880s memoir called *Shadows* that this was a "bright and respectable old place" blessed with an intellectual legacy as well as a thirst for new knowledge. He cited the *Banner of Light*, the abundance of healers and the varieties of séances as proof of the spiritual energy being generated. His glowing tribute stated: "One of the things that helps make me proud of this locality, that enhances its value to me, is the reception that it has given to modern Spiritualism." Boston offered a friendly setting from which to contemplate the spirit world.

BIBLIOGRAPHY

Annual Reports of the Town of Winchester. Boston: Alfred Mudge & Sons, 1872–78.
Banner of Light, 1857–95.
Barnum, Mary P. *Pierpont Genealogy and Connecting Lines.* Boston: James Allen Crosby, 1928.
Boston (City) Directory, 1850–80.
Boston Globe, 1872–1926.
Boston Investigator, 1879.
Brackett, Edward A. *Materialized Apparitions.* Boston: Gorham Press, 1908.
———. *The World We Live In.* Boston: Gorham Press, 1909.
Brackett, Herbert L. *Brackett Genealogy Part II: Descendants of Anthony Brackett of Portsmouth and Captain Richard Brackett of Braintree.* Washington, D.C.: H.L. Brackett, 1907.
Brown, E. Gerry. *Spiritual Scientist*, 1874–1878. Accessed on website for the International Association for the Preservation of Spiritualist and Occult Periodicals (IAPSOP).
Buckland, Thomas. *The Handbook of Mesmerism, for the Guidance and Instruction of All Person Who Desire to Practise Mesmerism for the Cure of Diseases, and to Alleviate the Sufferings of Their Fellow Creatures.* 2nd ed. London: Hippolyte Bailliere, 1850
Buescher, John B. *The Other Side of Salvation: Spiritualism and the Nineteenth-Century Religious Experience.* Boston: Skinner House Books, 2004.
Cambridge Chronicle (newspaper), 1840–80.

Capron, Eliab W. *Modern Spiritualism: Its Facts and Fanaticisms*. Boston: Bela Marsh, 1855.
Chapman, Henry Smith. *History of Winchester, Massachusetts*. Vol. 1. Hanover, MA: Halliday Lithograph Corporation, 1975.
Coffin, Charles Carlton. *The Story of the Great Fire*. Boston: Shepard and Gill, 1872.
Daily Alta California (newspaper), 1849–91.
Davenport, Reuben Briggs. *The Death-Blow to Spiritualism, Being the True Story of the Fox Family of Margaret Fox Kane and Catherine Fox Jencken*. New York: G.W. Dillingham, 1888.
Day, John W. *A Biographic Memorial of Luther Colby*. Boston: Banner of Light Publishing Company, 1895.
Dickens, Charles. *Household Words: A Weekly Journal*. Vol. XI. London: Ward, Lock and Tyler, 1855.
Dods, John Bovee. *The Philosophy of Mesmerism and Electrical Psychology*. Edited by J. Burns. London: James Burns Progressive Library, 1886.
Drake, Maud Eugenia Barrock Lord. *Psychic Light, the Continuity of Law and Life*. Kansas City, KS: Frank Riley, 1902.
Clubb, Henry S., ed. *Food, Home and Garden* 2, no. 16 (April 1898).
Fowler, O.S. *American Phrenological Journal and Miscellany* 10 (1848).
Frothingham, O.B. "Some Phases of Idealism in New England." *Atlantic Monthly* 52, no. 309 (July 1883).
———. *Theodore Parker: A Biography*. New York: G.P. Putnam's Sons, 1880.
Hardinge, Emma. *Modern American Spiritualism: A Twenty Years' Record of the Communion Between the Earth and the World of Spirits*. 2nd ed. New York: self-published, 1870.
Hayward, A.S. *Nature's Law in Human Life: An Exposition of Spiritualism*. Boston: William White and Company, 1872.
Houdini, Harry. *A Magician Among the Spirits*. New York: Harper & Brothers, 1924.
Marryat, Florence. *There Is No Death*. New York: Lovell, Coryell & Company, 1891.
Middleborough Gazette (newspaper). 1850.
New England Spiritualist (newspaper). 1855–57.
Newton, A.E, and S.J. Newton. *The "Ministry of Angels" Realized*. 2nd ed. Boston: A.E. Newton, 1853.
Newton, James A. "Crow's Nest or Eagles Aeries?" *Old-Time New England* 67, no. 3–4 (Winter/Spring 1977).
Parker, Theodore (spirit), and John W. Day. *Biography of Mrs. J. H. Conant, the World's Medium of the Nineteenth Century*. 2nd ed. Boston: William White and Company, 1873.
Providence Daily Journal (newspaper), 1884.

Putnam, Allen. *Flashes of Light from the Spirit-Land Through the Mediumship of Mrs. J.H. Conant.* Boston: William White and Company, 1872.

———. *Natty: A Spirit: His Portrait and His Life.* Boston: Bela Marsh, 1856.

———. *Post-Mortem Confessions: Being Letters Written Through a Mortal's Hand by Spirits Who, When in Mortal Were Officers of Harvard College.* Boston: Colby & Rich, 1886.

Redman, George A., MD. *Mystic Hours; Or Spiritual Experience.* Boston: Bela Marsh, 1859.

Report of the Proceedings of the Professed Spiritualist Agents and Mediums. Boston: Office of the Boston Courier, 1859.

Smolnikar, Andrew B. *Secret Enemies of True Republicanism.* Spring Hill, PA: Robert D. Eldridge Co., 1859.

Some Account of the Vampiers of Onset Past and Present. Boston: S. Woodbury Company, 1892.

Spiritual Philosopher (newspaper). 1850.

Spiritual Scientist (newspaper). 1875.

Stevens, William B. *History of Stoneham, Massachusetts.* Stoneham, MA: F.L. & W.E. Whittier, 1891.

Sunderland, LaRoy. *Confessions of a Magnitizer Exposed.* Boston: Kedding & Company, 1845.

Trowbridge, John T. "Miscellaneous Experiences." *Journal of the American Society for Psychical Research* 3 (1909).

Underhill, A. Leah. *The Missing Link in Modern Spiritualism.* New York: Thomas R. Knox & Co., 1885.

Wetherbee, John. *"Shadows": Being a Familiar Presentation of Thoughts and Experiences in Spiritual Matters, with Illustrative Narrations.* Boston: Colby & Rich, 1885.

Whitlock, L.L. *Facts: A Monthly Magazine Devoted to Mental and Spiritual Phenomena.* 1883–87.

Willis, Frederick L.H. "Dr. Willis Experiences." *Spiritual Magazine* 5 (n.d.).

Winchester Star (newspaper), 1906–08.

Wolfe, Napoleon Bonaparte, MD. *Startling Facts in Modern Spiritualism.* 2nd ed. Chicago: Religio-Philosophical Publishing House, 1875.

INDEX

A

Adams, Alvin 29, 30
Agassiz, Dr. 28, 30
Albro, George 96, 101
Allen, Reverend J. Madison 89
Allyn, Fannie 72, 88, 89
animals 55, 56, 57
Antietam 46, 86
Ayer, Hattie 103
Ayer, Marcellus 102

B

Baxter, Frank 72, 88
Berry, Gertrude 96, 102
Berry, Helen 80, 81, 96
Berry, William 23, 24, 25, 26, 45, 49, 108
Bethesda Institute 37
Black, James Wallace 36
Boston Fire of 1872 58
Boston Investigating Committee 28
Brackett, Edward A. 72, 77
Brown, John 44, 79

C

Cambridge 24, 25, 26, 27, 28, 29, 45, 71, 116
Chamberlain, Annie Lord 52
Channing, William Ellery 35
Charlestown 13, 15, 54, 58, 71, 76, 85
Chelsea 108
Coan, Ada 37
Colby, Luther 23, 24, 25, 34, 49, 62, 93, 94, 101, 108, 112
Conant, Fanny 23, 24, 45, 49, 50, 51, 55, 65, 108
Concannon, Oliver 105, 106
Cooper, Margaretta S. 11, 14
Cowen, Mrs. Amanda 82
Crandon, Margery 117
Crowell, Charles 49, 50

D

Davis, Andrew Jackson 13, 42
Dickens, Charles 21
Doten, Lizzie 37, 90
Dow, Moses A. 83
Doyle, Sir Arthur Conan 116

E

Edwards Congregational Church 17
Ewins, Mehitable 12

INDEX

F

Fay, Mrs. Herman 80
First Spiritual Temple 102
Forest Hills Cemetery 8, 45, 51, 57, 112, 118, 120, 127
Fox sisters 7, 13, 29, 30, 84

G

Gardner, Dr. Henry 28, 37

H

Hardinge, Emma 14, 43
Harvard 15, 26, 27, 28, 30, 32, 38, 39, 94, 116, 117
Hayden, Mrs. (Maria) 16, 18, 21
Hollis Street Church 32, 33, 114
Houdini, Harry 115
Hyde, Mrs. 35
Hyde Park 16

L

Lake, Mrs. 104
Lake Pleasant 74
Lincoln, Mary Todd 65
Lord, Maud E. 66

M

Mabel, Warren 84
Malden 12, 52
Mansfield, James V. 29, 30, 34, 35
Marryat, Mrs. 100
Marsh, Bela 21
materialization 80, 81, 98, 99, 100, 105, 106
Melrose 88
mesmerism 12, 33, 79, 81
Middleborough 89
Mumler, William H. 60, 85

N

Newton, Alonzo E. 17, 22
Newton, Sarah Jane 17, 18, 19, 20, 22, 80

P

Parker, Theodore 38, 41, 44, 50, 66, 108
Phrenology 79, 81
Pierpont, John 31, 32, 33, 35, 114
Plymouth 72, 89
Public Circles 25, 41, 44, 48, 50, 52, 55, 60, 65, 100, 114

R

Reading 38
Redman, George 17, 29
Rich, Issac B. 109
Ross, Mrs. Hannah 92, 119

S

Stoneham 71, 82
Sunderland, LaRoy 11, 39

T

Tappan, Minnie 50
Theatre, Exeter Street 107
Theatre, Hollis Street 112
Theatre, Keith, B.F. 115
Trowbridge, John T. 20, 22

W

Watertown 31, 49, 50
West Medford 33, 34
Wetherbee, John 81, 120
Whittier, Edward Tuck 85
Willis, Frederick 26
Winchester 71, 72, 73, 74, 76, 77, 80, 81, 82, 88, 92

ABOUT THE AUTHOR

Dee Morris is an independent scholar and educational consultant specializing in the nineteenth-century history of Greater Boston. She presents walking tours at Forest Hills Cemetery (Jamaica Plain) and programs at libraries, schools and historical societies. Her goal is to connect people with their civic ancestors.

Visit us at
www.historypress.net

This title is also available as an e-book